MW01675057

Unlocking Christ's Parables

A Guide For Applying The Wisdom Of Christ's Parables To Our Lives

TRUTHOUGHT™

P.O. Box 222
Roscoe, IL 61073

TRUTHOUGHT™

Published by Truthought™ Publications, Roscoe, Illinois, U.S.A. Truthought™ Publications is the publishing division of Truthought™, an organization active in preserving and promoting the truth of God and His character in the thoughts and lives of contemporary people.

ISBN 0-9653376-0-X

Printed in the U.S.A. by Morris Publishing

Library of Congress Catalog Card Number: 96-90621

TABLE OF CONTENTS

Foreword

What is good education? The answer to this question is too often determined by the resources and funding it takes to receive an education. The real answer, though, cannot be summed up in monetary terms, but should be defined by what that education ought to do once it has been received.

The first and most important obligation of education is to teach each new generation how to live responsibly and productively in their community. A free society cannot continue unless its members are self-disciplined, law-abiding, and willfully compliant with the informal codes of conduct that enable people to live and work together amicably and productively.

If a young person does not learn to be responsible, nothing else that is learned will make it possible to have a stable and satisfying life. Learning social responsibility, however, is only part of the process of receiving a good education.

It is equally important to learn the other elements of responsible living -- love of God, truthfulness, morality, piety, courtesy, cooperativeness, charity, fidelity to one's promises and the many other traits that foster healthy character.

Thus, to achieve the goals of a good education, the young must be trained not only in the social ideals that serve to shape healthy community but also to understand and cherish God and the principles that underlie the Christian faith. They must be taught so thoroughly that they will voluntarily subordinate other interests and desires, when necessary, in order that godly ideals may be sustained.

Truthought Publications are designed to teach the values that underlie this definition of a good education. Fostering biblically sound principles for responsible living, they do not simply "tell" what must be done, but carefully unfold "how and why" it should be done.

Each student is led to discover the necessity and process of responsibly living with regard for God and one another in all facets of life and, most importantly, at the center of God's will. Thus, life-changing and lasting impressions are made upon each individual character.

Rarely have I encountered contemporary educational materials that so clearly address and encompass the basic foundational principles so greatly needed for educating succeeding generations. I heartily recommend these study guides to parents, educators, and students alike, who are seeking to complete and preserve a truly good education for themselves and generations to come.

Carl E. Baugh, Ph.D.
Creation Evidence Museum
Glen Rose, Texas

Acknowledgments

For their participation in developing this study series, we are particularly grateful for the efforts of the Truthought Staff. Rogie Spon thoughtfully and prayerfully put together the concept, text and layout. Kelly Mullins' editorial strength brought vitality and refinement to the material. Dr. Rick Tingle organized field testing that provided practical hands-on awareness and polish in the final stages. The artistic skills of Tony Ross gave visual impact to the series covers. The feedback, patience and resource support of Robert Spon kept this project in motion to the finish.

We also want to express appreciation to the many friends who provided critical input and analysis during the development stages: Marty Zuniga, Ken Schultz, Jeff and Nancy Paul, Cherolyn Lexvold, Gary Kenner, Dean Harvey, Harry Conn and Jack Blackburn.

Introduction
Parable Paradigms

It is often said that the optimistic and naive "see the world through rose-colored glasses," meaning that their view of reality is tinted with a cheerful but unrealistic cast. The reverse could be said of those with cynical outlooks; they see the world through dim colored glasses. Paradigms are like eyeglasses through which we view information, make decisions and take action.

The "paradigm eyeglasses" we look through to analyze information and determine its accuracy are made from presuppositions. Presuppositions are formed from what we learn and experience. The correctness of our presuppositions determines the accuracy of our paradigm, our world view. Thus, not all paradigms are beneficial. Distorted paradigms can be tragic. Fortunately, we can and do make paradigm shifts throughout our lives, always progressing toward a more accurate and complete world view.

Landmark, scientific breakthroughs which are the result of breaks with wrong presuppositions are good examples of paradigm shifts; such as, the discovery that the world is not flat but spherical or that the sun does not revolve around the earth, but rather the earth revolves around the sun.

Like scientific breakthroughs, every major revival in the history of Christianity has resulted from a break with wrong religious presuppositions, a break with inaccurate traditions and thoughts of the religious orthodoxy of the day.

Whenever we change a presupposition, whether religious or otherwise, we shift our paradigm. Whether these shifts are positive, negative, instant or developmental, they move us from one way of perceiving reality, to another. Paradigm shifts create powerful change, because our world view, right or wrong, is the source of our attitudes and behaviors, and most importantly, our relationship with God.

Adam and Eve were the first to make a wrong paradigm shift. In the garden, God let them enjoy all of life's good things without toil or labor. He gave them only one simple law, and that was *not to eat of the fruit of the tree of the knowledge of good and evil.*

It seems ridiculous that this little rule was too difficult, too burdensome for them to follow. God even gave them the powerful incentive of life for keeping the simple, little rule. So Adam and Eve understood the one and only little commandment God had given them to follow, and they had no trouble keeping it for a time: then Satan presented Eve with a different idea concerning the result of eating the forbidden fruit. He said, "In the day you eat of it you shall not die but will have the wisdom of life and death and good and evil and be like God."

After what seems very little consideration, Eve discarded her original presuppositions based on what God had told her and replaced them with new presuppositions based on what Satan had told her, resulting in a paradigm shift, a new world view.

The shift was a *wrong* one! The paradigm presented to Eve by Satan was a *half-truth.* It was true that when Adam and Eve ate the fruit they had the knowledge of good and evil, but they did not have the equivalent knowledge of God and they did not become like Him in that sense, as promised. Adam and Eve did not die physically, at least not immediately when they ate the fruit, but they did die spiritually and eventually they died physically too.

It did not take Adam and Eve long to realize their mistake and, most likely, they quickly adjusted their thinking back to their original presuppositions and paradigm. However, the consequences of their action could not be shifted as easily as their paradigm, sadly the world is still affected by their action.

History has repeated itself. Interpreting God's Word through false presuppositions is the most common mistake throughout the history of Judeo-Christian religion. It is like trying to see the world through glasses that are the wrong prescription: everything is distorted to some degree.

For us, the way we perceive God depends largely upon the presuppositions we hold when we encounter His Word, the presuppositions our family, teachers, pastors and friends pass on to us. Thus, our frequent error is to view God, Christianity and the Bible through a faulty, pre-existing paradigm built from other sources rather than making God's Word the primary paradigm through which we sift all information,

God is the *a priori* to everything and His Word is the perfect paradigm for all things pertaining to life, in other words, a world view based on reality (2 Peter 1). We must avoid relying on governments, businesses, schools, churches, even family or friends as paradigms for analyzing the Word of God to see if It is true. Rather, we must always shed the light of the Word of God on these sources of influence and information to determine whether these correspond to Truth.

We find in the New Testament that Jesus frequently used parables when teaching. His Parables are appropriate to our discussion of paradigms because Jesus intended them to be used by us as perfect paradigms for analyzing our world view to determine whether it is accurate. Christ's parables are like perfectly prescribed and ground eyeglasses through which we can sift our thoughts concerning God, ourselves, and others, and see if our beliefs are accurate, and if not, how we can adjust them correctly.

Part I

Comprehending The Key Parable

1
The Key To Unlock Christ's Parables

Because Christ's parables make up one-third of His recorded teachings, accurate interpretation of them is crucial, since otherwise we are certain to misunderstand 33 percent of what He taught.

Jesus' parables require a special key, one which does not unlock the meaning of any part of Scripture other than the parables told by Him. Jesus Himself implied that without this key we will likely misunderstand all of His parables (Mark 4:13).

The key is not difficult to find: it is the first parable, *The Parable of the Sower.* Jesus' parables cannot be fully comprehended without an accurate understanding of this first one, recorded in Mark 4:1-20, Luke 8:4 -15, and Matthew 13:1-23.

Until now, we may have casually skimmed over the parables focusing on any number of them before giving attention to the first one. Thus, we may have grasped a partial interpretation, but partial understanding of what Jesus taught is far from adequate. In order to comprehend all of the parables one must unlock the door to understanding and enter through the doorway. That doorway is the *Parable of the Sower.*

We could say that the *Parable of the Sower* is the paradigm parable through which we must sift all of Christ's other parables in order to interpret them accurately. The parables are important to us because they are intended to show us how to live (and how not to live) the Christian Life and how to spread (and how not to spread) that Life to others. These things, manner of life and manner of teaching, are the central focus of this study.

1. Read the *Points on Parables, Appendix* at the back of this study booklet before going further. You will find pertinent information concerning parables that will aid you in answering the following questions.

2. **What is the special key to unlock the meaning of the parables told by Jesus? What scripture gives evidence of this?**

3. **Why should we shun popular interpretations and applications?**

4. **What two opposite accomplishments did Jesus achieve in His parables?**

2

The Use of The Key Parable in Christ's Ministry

Jesus preferred teaching in parables when addressing large crowds (Mark 4:11, 12). He wanted to conceal spiritual truth from those who were indifferent, apathetic or in opposition to it, but reveal it to those who were ready and worthy. Teaching in parables was the best method for accomplishing both of these goals at once.

In contrast to His technique when teaching crowds, Jesus was direct when teaching His disciples. Often, far away from the clamor, after the crowd had dwindled and the setting was more intimate, He explained His parables to them in plain terms (Mark 4:33, 34).

To thoroughly understand Jesus' objective we must realize that He was in no sense being partial or exclusive by sharing the hidden meaning with His disciples. A careful look at scripture shows He did not exclude others from the advantages of direct interpretation, but welcomed any who lingered to learn with an honest heart (Mark 4:10). His purpose in using parables was to veil the truth from the insincere, lazy, indifferent and strongly opposed -- in no way was he being arrogant or showing favoritism. He simply intended to reveal the truth only to the degree in which each individual would agree with it and apply it. Thus his parables hid the truth from those who would abuse it while imparting it to those who honestly wanted to follow it. The design of His parables was to conceal truth from the unreceptive while revealing it to the receptive.

Read *The Parable of The Sower,* Mark 4:1-20

1. **Describe the setting in which Jesus is teaching.**

2. What are the four types of soil on which the sower sows?

3. Reread verse 10. Was it only to the 12 disciples that Jesus revealed the meaning of His parable? Why do you think He let these others in on the meaning too?

4. If you had heard Jesus teach, would you have caught a glimpse of truth and re-mained for more, or would you have gone away without caring for an interpretation? Explain.

5. What dual purpose did Jesus accomplish with His parables?

3
The Heart

In this chapter you will be doing less reading and more personal discovery beginning by finding the answers to the questions in the opposite column. You will want to begin now with the first question and work your way through question 3 then begin reading in this column again until you come to the next group of questions in the opposite column. This is the study pattern you will follow throughout this workbook.

Read Mark 4:1-20

1. **What are the four types of soil on which the sower sows?**

2. **Reread verses 10-12 of Mark 4. How do you feel about this statement from Jesus? Does it seem fair? Why or Why not?**

3. **There is yet another symbol to be uncovered. It is referred to only in Luke but strongly implied in the other 2 gospel accounts. See if you can pin-point it in Luke 8:15.**

Regardless of the characteristics (stony, thorny or good), the "soil" which takes hold of the seed symbolizes a person's *heart.*

But what is meant by a person's *heart* in this sense? We can be sure it is not the physical, blood-pumping, organ of the body, but something equally vital to life: spirituality.

By reviewing some scripture we can learn more about the *heart* as found in the Bible.

4. Look up each of the following verses and explain what you think the *heart* means in each.
   Proverbs 21:2;
   Proverbs 4:23 (*Compare this to keeping a field or crop for harvest.)*;
   Deut. 8:2;
   Matthew 6:21;
   Matthew 13:44

5. Continue the above exercise with Matthew 12: 33-35.

As you answered questions 4 and 5 did you notice the urgent focus on getting the treasure in the field? The one who found it never thought he should work until he earned enough to purchase the field. Instead, without delay, he sold all that he had in order to buy it immediately.

Everything around us (the world) is geared to seduce us into selfishness, giving second place to "the treasure hidden in the field." But this wise person *urgently* focused on true value because that was where his heart was.

In those passages above, the words *heart* and *treasure* are synonyms and can be used interchangeably. Note that the good person brings forth good things from his heart (his treasure) and the evil person brings forth evil things from his heart (his treasure). The heart and treasure are the same.

Though we have reviewed only a little about the word heart in Scripture, we have gained a general understanding of its meaning in the context of this parable.

The following *heart* illustration will help pull the concept together.

The Career vs. The Goal

Two young men of similar backgrounds have decided to become pastors. To achieve their goal both young men complete Bible College and enroll in seminary and both purchase new Bibles, books and materials to complete their education. Each young man takes the same steps toward becoming a pastor. Yet one of them truly wants to live his life for God while the other wants to live his life for himself.

Their ultimate intentions, that is, their supreme motivations, are opposite, even though their choices and actions are identical. The second young man's heart is true to his visible goals and God. But, the heart of the first young man is centered on the fulfillment of self-centered dreams. He is hungry for power, thirsty for recognition, and fancies speaking eloquently to large audiences. He hopes, with little effort, to satisfy his lusts through a career as a pastor. He realizes he must undergo some preparation, but reasons it will be worth it in the long run.

The first young man is producing corrupt fruit (deceitful) while the second young man is producing good fruit (honest), each after the manner of his own heart. Yet both men, from the outside, appear to have equally worthy intentions in their career goals because their subordinate choices and actions are the same -- they look alike. The strategic difference lies hidden within the primary motive of their individual hearts.

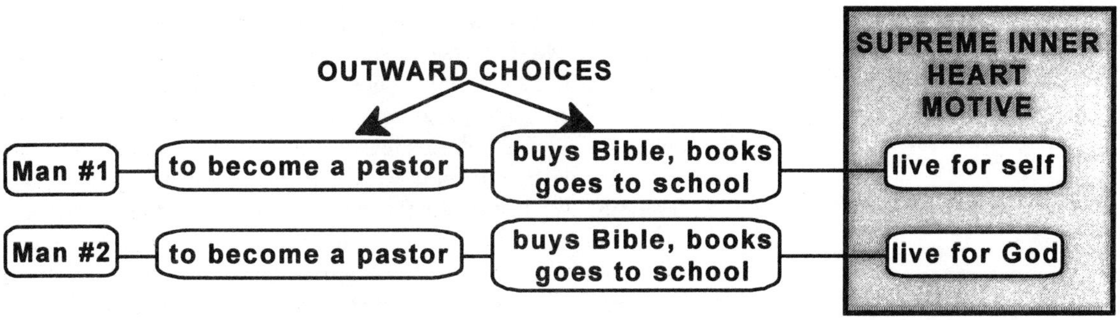

The word *heart*, the terms *ultimate intention*, *supreme motive*, all refer to the drive behind individual personalities. Our hearts determine our course in life, it is the helm of reasoning that determines our action.

The *heart* in scripture is occasionally translated as *innermost being*, or *mind*, and sometimes as *determination of will.* In Proverbs 21:2 we read, "all deeds are right in the sight of the doer but the Lord weighs the heart." This means it is God Who analyzes heart motives.

Our *heart* is the seat of our affections, the core of our purpose for living, all of our actions and choices in life stem from the heart.[1] Whether those actions are out of a supreme love for God and fellow man, or a supreme love for self, it is all hidden deep within one's heart.

6. **Look up Ezekiel 18:31. Now, remembering all that you have learned regarding the *heart*, rewrite Ezekiel 18:31 in your own words, (try to avoid using the word *heart*).**

The portion of Ezekiel 18:31,"make for yourself a new heart," simply means to have a new purpose for living--Christ. This new purpose for living is always followed by a new manner of living. With this *new manner* in mind, Christ drew the parallels between the various types of soils, comparing them to human hearts, because it is the *condition of heart* that produces a *new manner of living* just as the *condition of soil* is responsible for the amount of fruit or lack of it.

---

1. Right action can only follow right understanding. If our supreme goal is to love God then we do not need to monitor our conduct each moment of the day. When we make choices everyday that to the best of our understanding are in line with God's purpose for our lives, and we find we are mistaken, this is not sin. It is the one who *knows* to do good and does not do it that sins (James 4:17). God holds us responsible for what we understand and know, not what we do not know (Deut. 29:29). Our courts use the same considerations. While it is safe to pardon one who erred unintentionally, it is a danger to the public when one guilty of intentional harm is released. The motives and intentions are the determining factor. Clearly it is possible to have a pure intention of heart yet accidentally make mistakes. Thank God for his mercy and grace in judgment. He holds us accountable only for what we understand (including our desire to understand). He judges and acquits us according to our relationship with His Son and our purity of motive rather than perfection of conduct.

The next four chapters are devoted to the four different soils and the manner in which the sower spreads his seed. There is one chapter for each section of the parable. Each chapter contains a section examining the soil and a section examining the sower. The objective in these chapters is to collectively determine the parables' scriptural interpretation and its focus as a whole.

4

Sowing along the Path

This chapter, like the previous chapter, begins by letting you gather information through personal discovery rather than simply reading. Please begin by answering the questions in the opposite column and following the same procedure as you did in the last chapter. This will be the last time these instructions are provided for you so be sure you remember them in following chapters.

Section I : The Soil of the Path

Read The Parable in Mark 4. give special attention to verses 3 through 5, and 14, 15.

1. Look up Luke chapter 8 and read verses 11 and 12. What is the seed?

2. What becomes of seed sown on the path? What is the final result of sowing seed in soil of this kind?

3. Did the hearts symbolized by the soil on the path ever believe and experience salvation (new life in Christ)?

4. Sometimes it is suggested that those sown along the path are backslidden Christians who have lost their *communion* but not their *union* with Christ. What does this portion of the parable suggest about the teaching that backslidden Christians have lost communion but not union with Christ?

5. Review Mark 4 verse 15. Why weren't the hearts symbolized by the soil on the path saved?

The devil stole away the seed that fell along the path: this is true. Yet, this answer alone is uncomfortable. Does it mean that upon hearing God's word we are randomly left at Satan's disposal to have the Word stolen from our hearts? It runs contrary to logic that a loving, powerful God would allow such a devilish scheme to be carried out after the planting of His Word.

6. Read Isaiah 55:10,11. Do you think this contradicts what we have just read about seed (the Word) sown along the path? Why or why not?

7. Look up Matthew 13:18, 19. Can you find the missing piece to this puzzle? Why weren't the hearts symbolized by the soil on the path able to believe and receive the Word? Why were they such easy prey for the devil to steal the seed.

8. Throughout the gospels Jesus repeatedly exhorts his hearers to listen (fifteen times Christ calls attention to certain statements). Carefully read the author's paraphrase of Mark 4:23-25 in the opposite column.

"Let anyone with ears to hear listen!" and He said to them, "Pay attention to what you hear; the measure you give [of attention] will be the measure you get [in understanding], and still more [understanding] will be given you. For to those who have [understanding] more [understanding] will be given; and from those who have nothing [no understanding], even what [little comprehension] they have will be taken away." (Bracketed words added for emphasis and clarity).

9. To clarify the meaning of the verses to the left read Matthew 13:10-17. Next, look up Hebrews 2:1, 3 and 3:15. What are all of these verses intended to emphasize?

Comprehension of the Gospel is imperative to salvation. "Let anyone with ears to hear listen..." is much more than casual advice to stop day-dreaming and pay attention. It is crucial instruction for finding new life in Christ!

The fact, too often overlooked, is that no person can believe what he or she does not understand. In other words, one cannot "accept in the heart" what one's mind rejects, misunderstands, or is indifferent to.

What do we mean by acceptance in the heart? True acceptance of Christ's message, or any other message, is generated from one's freewill. This belief should be based upon accurate information, and the choice of the believer should be made without his being overly influenced by emotion. For true belief and commitment to occur there may be no duress, force, bribery, or extortion, and as little appeals to selfish interests as possible. (Appeals to selfish interests would include encouragement to believe in Christ for the sole purpose of avoiding hell to spend eternity in heaven.)

10. How did Jesus sum up the problem with seed sown on the path in Matthew 13:19?

11. The logical question, then, is why didn't the people symbolized in this section of the parable understand? The most obvious answer lies in their character. As an exercise, list some of the characteristics of an actual path.

12. Compare these characteristics to the sort of people Jesus is referring to when He speaks of "seed sown on the path." How are they alike?

The fact that these people were not interested in listening is the most apparent reason that many were unable to understand, but not the only reason. To learn more about the reason for their lack of comprehension we must examine the responsibility of the sower.

Section II: The Responsibility of the Sower, Who Sows along the Path

1. Review the definition of a parable (Appendix I). Does sowing seed along a path seem like a good farming procedure?" Why or why not?

Sowing seed along a path would not have seemed as strange to those hearing this parable in Jesus' day as it does to us. Then, it was common to find major thoroughfares cutting across a farmer's field. This does not mean, though, that a farmer would intentionally sow seed directly on that path! He would try to avoid wasting seed on the pathways and concentrate on keeping it in the field.

Some theologians have offered another cultural solution. Though it may appears to us as bad farming, it was farming custom in biblical times to sow before plowing. This would suggest that the sower sows purposely on the path because he is intending to plow over it later.

2. Look at verse 5 of Mark 4. What happens to the seed along the path?

We learned earlier that the correct interpretation of a parable is found only when that interpretation leaves none of the circumstances unexplained. For this reason other scholars disagree with the previous conclusion. Even though the standard practice was to plow after seed was sown, at least half of the seed, according to the parable, was scattered in places that would be difficult to plow. One cannot plow a road and continue to use it; one cannot plow rocky ground; and plowing where the seed fell on thorns would produce undesirable results. There is something odd about the way the sower in the parable sows, and it is reinforced by the fact that so many have felt it necessary to attempt to explain his method. Their straining only serves to highlight the fact that his method leaves us with questions.

The questions that we would seek to solve concerning the sower's act of sowing along the path are:

(a) Why, when parables typically consist of practical-life-examples, did Jesus use what has been called an odd illustration, such as sowing on a path?

(b) How should we interpret the sower's action of sowing on the path?

3. Read, again, verse 11 of Luke 8. Since the seed represents the Word of God, what sort of person must the sower represent?

Sowing seed on a path becomes more relevant when the sower's technique is viewed as a typical way many Christians spread the gospel today. They barely seem to understand what they are talking about and do not seem to care much whether anyone else does either.

Superficial gospel presentations are often attempts to make money or to bask in the attention of center stage. Others, like the farmer in our parable, are too naive and careless to avoid sowing on the path. For these it is a matter of quantity not quality. They present the gospel and solicit prayers of faith like assembly-line workers racing to see who can punch-out the most product in the least time, but are careless about quality. This careless method is often observed in door-to-door and telemarketing evangelism programs where the presentation is rapid, designed to persuade people to make decisions quickly without checking whether they actually understand their decisions.

All of us have heard ambiguous, offensive, pseudo-presentations of the gospel. In the *Parable of the Sower*, Jesus is saying that the result of these presentations is the same as sowing on a path: a crop is never harvested due to the sower's lax method, the hearer's indifference or both (but it has nothing to do with the seed -- Word of God).

When the sower presents a pseudo-gospel or is too lazy to make sure his hearers understand, it is no fault of the hearers. How could anyone be held accountable for understanding the gospel when his closest encounter has been a shallow, misrepresentation?

Imagine the famous American evangelist, Billy Graham, addressing a large auditorium filled with Japanese students. An interpreter fluent in the Japanese language would be needed to assist him. If you have never had this experience you may be surprised to find that it is easier than speaking to an audience that needs no interpretation. With an interpreter, the speaker reels off a few short statements then pauses while the interpreter repeats the matter in the language of the audience. This gives the lecturer time to think during the pauses.

Now suppose Mr. Graham spoke on for 30 minutes without pausing for interpretation then abruptly stopped and said to the interpreter, "Please ask this group what they think of my sermon so far and whether they believe it to be true. Then tell them I want them to get up out of their seats and come forward to make a decision..." The response from the crowd would be, "How does this fellow expect us to take his statements to heart when we haven't understood a word he has said!?"

The Gospel must be presented in a way that the listeners can comprehend before they can be expected to understand and believe.

We are glad that Rev. Graham has not been known to preach without pausing for an interpretation in other languages. But many Christians present the Gospel, even to those who speak their own language, in ways that do not make sense or cannot be understood.

The pseudo-gospel presentation that develops urgent emotion in the listener but fails to give birth to valid understanding renders the hearer's response useless and void of life-giving power.

Luke 8:12 and Matthew 13:19 plainly show that those along the path were never saved because of superficial, inaccurate presentations of the gospel or because they did not care enough to dig out the truth and conditions of salvation for themselves.

4. Earlier we read the solution offered by some scholars that the sower sowing on the path intended to plow over it later. What does this solution imply about the sower?

5. How many of us, who call ourselves "Christian," fall under the category of being a "sower?" Is any Christian exempt from the task of spreading the Word? Why or why not?

6. Not all are called to be evangelists but all Christians are called upon to be witnesses, even if only by example. Does being a witness in example alone qualify as "sowing?" Why or why not?

7. List 2 reasons that explain why those along the path were unable to become Christians.

5

Sowing on Rocky Ground

Section 1: The Rocky Soil

1. Read Mark 4:5-17.

In our home, maybe like yours, we have a large supply of rubber bands that we don't need and rarely use. This is because we take the local newspaper and when it arrives every day we roll-off the rubber band binding the paper and drop it in a nearby drawer. We have done this for so long it has become automatic. Obviously we don't subscribe to the newspaper so we can stock-up on rubber bands; storing them is just a simple response to receiving the paper. A similar response resulted in many stone fences seen in the Eastern United

...t of the USA you will notice mile ... stone fences. The purpose of a ...ep animals in or out, or for privacy, ...astern fences were built primarily ...needed to be removed from the soil so ...rass could be planted. Stacking rows ...ecessary means of preparing the ...g -- the stones as fences served a lesser ...mary purpose was to prepare the ... removing the stones.

2. Practically speaking, rocks hinder plowing, but what else made the land useless for planting while the stones remained? (Refer to verses 5 and 6, then 16 and 17 of Mark chapter 4).

Rocks are a tremendous barrier to plant growth and a serious hindrance to crop production as noted in verses 5, 6, 16 and 17 of Mark chapter 4.

We have already learned in the parable of the sower that the seed represents the Word of God, or the Gospel, and the sower represents Christians, while the various soils represent those that come in contact with the Gospel through the effort of a Christian. In this parable, then, we can determine by their very nature that the stones represent unyielded barriers that hinder growth in the hearer's life.

Jesus invites us to come to Him as we are, like untilled ground full of stones, but He insists we repent, that we have a change of heart about our lifestyle.

Like the farmer who has acquired fallow ground, Jesus receives us in our present condition at the time we hear the Gospel and are called to new life, but He reserves the right to transform us once we commit to becoming His children.

Wrong attitudes and behaviors are stones that must be dislodged. The conviction of sin is an acute awareness that we must eliminate and change attitudes and behaviors and make attempts at restitution when appropriate. The solution does not begin and end at the initial point of salvation. It is a process referred to as Christian transformation. (Titus 3:5, 6).

After Christ enters and receives possession of our lives, He continues to point out more and more stones that hurt us, others, and His Kingdom. As He shows us these stones and we remove them, we continue to grow. If Jesus showed us all of our moral pebbles and rocks at one time, we would likely "faint or die of despair" short of reaching the Cross (Psalms 27:13). That is why He so patiently and kindly reserves many stones for our future attention rather than overwhelming us all at once.

Once Christ reveals a stone, obedience is never optional, it is always mandatory. In other words, obedience must be consistently progressive and rarely regressive over the course of Christian experience.

God requires us to obey what little we know upon conversion. Then gradually, as we become fit for further enlightenment, He points to more areas we must change. This is the process of Christian transformation that takes place instantly and progressively continues throughout our lives. Simply put, sanctification begins at an actual point in time, but it is progressive (rarely, if ever, regressive) and life-long from that point on.

3. Read Hebrews 12: 3-12.

4. Look up Isaiah 55:6,7. Next, look up the word *forsake* in the dictionary. What does it mean "to forsake wicked ways and unrighteous thoughts?" What does God promise to those who do this?

5. What do you think the results would be for someone who refused to allow the stones to be removed from his heart?

6. What would the results be for someone who quickly yielded up those stones?

7. The key to eliminating the rocks can be found in James 4:17. In your own words explain what this verse means, especially "Anyone who knows the right thing to do..."

8. Apply this principle to "one who does not know the right thing to do."

9. How important is one's conscience in becoming holy as God requires, in other words, removing stones, and why? (Hebrews 9:14)?

10. Look up I Timothy 1:5-8, 18-20. What happens when we ignore our conscience and refuse to grow in understanding of right and wrong?

11. Is this the same as refusing to let go of "stones," in other words, not yielding to God in areas He has revealed?

12. Can you think of any stones in your life you have been avoiding that you needto yield to God? If so, what are you going to do about it?

13. What about stones God has yet to reveal, stones one is unaware of, is a person responsible for yielding up these? Why or why not?

14. Do you think God would allow any of His children to grow beyond what he is willing to learn and obey? Why or why not?

If the seed sown on the path symbolizes those who do not allow the Seed or Word to become embedded in their hearts, this category, rocky ground, indicates those who have a shallow hold upon the truth.

Rocky places often lay undetected beneath thin layers of soil making it impossible for the Seed to penetrate and firmly root. In the midst of the church we have far too many rocky hearts. What a difference they would make if the rocks were removed and the soil made deep and soft.

In our parable, God revealed unyielded areas (stones) but those in whom the seed was planted on stony ground refused to yield those areas up to Him -- they refused to progressively live up to the light they had been shown.

Once stones have been revealed to us by God but left in the soil, unyielded, the terrible result is that they damn our souls.

God will not give any of us the grace to grow spiritually beyond what we are *willing* to obey or how far we are *willing* to grow--to do so would only reinforce our negligence and disobedience. We must avoid circling the same rocks again and again; habitual sin leads to frustration and defeat. Yield up every revealed stone. Live up to all the light He gives you. Check yourself, be sure you want to please Him because you truly love Him; not just to pave a way for yourself into heaven. This is the love God deeply yearns for from us.

Section II: The Responsibility of the Sower Who Sows on Stony Ground

In this portion of the parable, the soil must yield the stones, but the sower has a responsibility to encourage that yielding. An illustration of the "stone-removing-process" in Christian growth is found in the nature of a marriage relationship. Consider the following fictitious engagement proposal.

The Proposal

A young Christian man who has been away at college for four years is approaching graduation and begins contemplating plans for the future.

After many weeks of thoughtful consideration and prayer he hops in his car and drives all night back to his home town where he wastes no time in heading for his high school sweetheart's home. As he pulls into the driveway his mind is filled with joyous anticipation. His step is spry as he leaps from his car and heads for the front door. He rings the bell and the seconds seem to lag as he rocks on his heels waiting for someone to answer. The door finally opens to reveal the girl he has driven so far to see.

He crosses the threshold and drops to one knee, pauses, then says, "Darling, I've thought and prayed for many days and I've driven all night to ask you if you will be my wife and share your life with me?"

Laughing, she replies, "Nothing could make me happier. I accept."

He follows her into the living room and together they sit and begin discussing all their plans for the future. He tells her about the fantastic job he has secured for himself after graduation in a city only 150 miles away. But she likes their home town and even though he has a job lined-up elsewhere, she wants to stay there. After all, she has a job herself and doesn't want to give that up.

Surprisingly, he is quick to concede, "That's OK, Honey, we'll stay here. You will still marry me, won't you?"

Soon it becomes painfully apparent that in his absence she has also made a few new friends -- all male, but none serious, of course, -- so she agrees to stop dating all of them except two of whom she is particularly fond.

"Oh, that's OK, I guess... You will still marry me anyway, won't you?" he pleads.

She thinks he should know one more thing. Since he's been away she has become involved in some "harmless social drinking and recreational drugs" but only now and then at after-hour-office-parties. She knows he wouldn't approve or join her in these activities, but insists on participating at least on weekends and holidays.

Staunchly holding forth his proposal he blurts, "Well, that's OK too, if only you will apologize and tell me you are sorry every time you get involved. Now, you will still marry me anyway, won't you?..."

1. Does this sound like ideal circumstances for marriage? Why or why not?

2. What feelings and thoughts did you have as you read this story?

3. What is your impression of the young man as he continues to propose?

4. What impression do you have of the young woman?

Far-fetched engagement story? Maybe so, but just like the farmer who sowed seed on a path, this analogy seems ridiculous at first, but in the context of our parable it is not so unrealistic after all. In fact, this type of "proposal scene" is typical when likened to the average Gospel invitation and the resulting marriage commitment of many to Christ. The pseudo-presentation passing for the Gospel today is: "You can keep your sin, you can have all of this and heaven too, but won't you please accept Jesus?"

This "gospel proposal" portrays Jesus much the same as the young man who will allow any blemish of character behavior to remain in his fiancée if she will only consent to marry him.

The result is people who want enough of Jesus to get to heaven when they die, but not enough to change their life here and now.

5. Look up Rev. 21:2, 9 and John 3:27-29. To whom do these verses point as being the Bride? And Who, according to these verses, is the Bridegroom?

6. Can you think of different ways the gospel may be presented that might lead others to believe they could have the type of marriage with Christ that was depicted in the engagement story? What key ingredients do you think were missing in the presentation of the gospel that would lead to this impression?

7. The little engagement story showed many signs of a risky marriage. Why do you think so many present the gospel as if the same signs make sense in one's relationship with Christ?

A change of heart about wrong attitudes and behavior and the desire to forsake them is what the Bible refers to as repentance. Simply put, repentance is yielding-up the "stones" in the soil of our hearts. Such willingness is the first non-optional condition to new and abundant life in Christ.

However, for many Christians the mere thought of putting conditions on the Gospel is a major obstacle. They fear that claiming salvation has conditions is preaching *works*. "Works" and "conditions," however, are poles apart. Works require action, such as, helping a little, old lady cross the street. Conditions are the opposite and require no action, such as, the condition that a shoplifter on parole, steal no more. When the shoplifter complies with parole and steals no longer, what has he done? He has not done anything. Instead, the act of stealing has ceased, no action has taken place, and the former shoplifter is no longer a shoplifter.

Refraining from wrong behavior as a result of repentance is the evidence of meeting the conditions of salvation. It is not works.

Often an argument is heard among Christians and stated something like this: "No one has to do anything to be a Christian other than believe." This is true, but only when one realizes that the meaning of "believe" in the Greek text means "to live in accordance with!" Believing faith is more than "thinking hard or agreeing heartily," it is "living in accordance with" and that is doing something, but it is not works. Works is any attempt to make reconciliation with God by any means other than the atoning work of Christ!

We can measure the difference between performing works and meeting conditions by looking at an example. Read the following story then answer the questions after it.

Meeting Conditions vs. Works

The Conrads were a typical suburban American family living in the North Lake Shore community near Chicago. They had two daughters and a son, Jenny, Rebecca, and Scott. The eldest, Jenny, was a few months from her sixteenth birthday and in the last week of her driver's education course. She had been pleading with her father to buy her a car and those pleas were growing stronger and more frequent as her birthday drew closer.

Jenny's father, Jim, was a pleasant quiet man, an architect and level-headed husband and father.

For weeks, Jim had been mulling over the idea of a car for Jenny. The money wasn't a problem, he just wanted to be sure that providing a car for Jenny was indeed the best decision.

A car is a big responsibility and a kid could get into all kinds of trouble with the freedom a car provides. Yet Jenny was a good girl -- dependable, cheerful, never a problem. But it would not be long before Jenny's brother and sister were legal driving age too and Jim didn't want to set a precedent he couldn't easily change if it was necessary later.

Rebecca and Scott were both more mischievous and Scott was especially prone to disobey. Jim didn't want to be called "unfair" if he decided either of the younger two kids were not responsible enough for a car. That decision would be made for their safety, not fairness, but Jim knew kids weren't always receptive to the wisdom in parental decisions.

Jim thought, perhaps, Jenny could go to work and earn the money to buy herself a car. Then his wife reminded him that Jenny was involved in the debate club, cheer-leading, and student government on top of her regular school work. Surely these activities were more beneficial for her right now than selling shoes or serving hamburgers.

Jim's wife was right, it would not be in Jenny's best interest to get a job and work to earn her car, besides she could not possibly save enough to buy a new car and Jim didn't want her on the road in some unsafe old clunker.

On the other hand, Jim thought it might be ideal for Scott to go to work and earn a car when he turned sixteen, especially if his behavior and attitude didn't improve between now and then. Plus, if Scott bought an old clunker he might learn something about mechanics.

Jim and his wife, Sarah, began to pray that God would help them come up with a solution suitable for the good of *all* their children. Then one night as Jim reclined in his favorite chair he came up with an answer. He would provide a car for his kids if each of them would meet certain conditions.

Those conditions would be that each child be of legal driving age, pass the state driver's examination, and maintain an above average grade point in school. Each of them also must fulfill certain responsibilities at home, and each of them must read at least 5 out of a list of 10 books that Jim and his wife recommended, then give their parents a verbal report on each.

(Jim and Sarah were avid readers and knew of many interesting novels that would help instill sound character in their children. Why not use a car as an incentive to get their children to read more, it couldn't hurt, in fact, it could only benefit them in the long run.)

Jim and Sarah agreed that if any of their children did not meet their conditions then that child could go to work and earn his or her own money to buy a car, or do without one.

8. In this story about the Conrad family, What choice could the children make concerning a car that would be considered *works*?

9. What choice would be *meeting the conditions*?

10. If the children choose *works* to get a car, how will it be provided?

11. How will the car be provided if the children choose to meet the conditions rather than getting a job?

12. Which choice would be more difficult for the Conrad children, [Circle your answer, either (a) or (b)].

a) getting a job, working, and saving their earnings to buy a car.
b)meeting their parents' conditions.

13. Which would be more difficult for a person who desires to be reconciled to God?

a) Living an absolutely sinless, unselfish life from birth to death.
b) repenting from sin; exercising faith in Jesus; and continuing in the love of God through obedience to Him.

14. Describe the difference between works and conditions.

15. God places conditions on salvation--repentance from sin, faith in Christ and continuing in love with God. Describe what *meeting these conditions* means, especially continuing in the love of God.

When Jesus died and rose again He became the *provision* for forgiveness of sins that we might be restored to a right relationship with God, con-sidering we meet the *conditions*, which are repentance from sin and obedience which is faith toward our Lord Jesus Christ and continuance in love for God.

True repentance results in a change of heart toward sin, the "stones" in our life, and we receive grace through faith in Christ to progressively eliminate those stones as He brings them to our attention.

Had it not been for Christ's life, death and resurrection as provision for those who choose to meet the conditions of faith, repentance, and continuance, we would have no alternative but to work to earn God's approval strictly by our own merit and strength. Then, if we did not meet sinless criteria in every instance of our life (and no one has, Romans 3:10, 23) we would remain eternally separated from Him.

In the first section of this chapter we examined the heart symbolized by stony ground. In the second section, we looked at ways and reasons the gospel is presented that give hearers reason to believe they do not need to rid their lives of sin.

6

Sowing Among Thorns

Section I: The Thorny Ground

When forced to respond to reality, it is the nature of those whose hearts are symbolized by thorns to shrink from God-dependent faith, especially when personal comfort, pleasures, lifestyle, or safety are threatened.

In order to clearly understand what is portrayed by the 'seed sown among thorns' we can first review an incident concerning the Israelites in Kadesh-Barnea.

1. Read Numbers chapter 13. Then, read the summary in the opposite column.

The Minority Report

Having arrived at the southern border of the promised land in a place called Kadesh Barnea, Moses appointed twelve elders to cross the border and spy out the land before leading the Children of Israel into their new homeland.

When the twelve returned, their report was dismal -- any good points had been completely forgotten after seeing the enormous race of people living in the land.

Moses' disappointment in their report must have been obvious, he knew God had never failed to give them victory and did not understand why they were so afraid.

But the spies insisted, "No, Moses, you don't understand, these people are huge, we felt like grasshoppers next to them."

Only Caleb and Joshua stood in disagreement saying, "Wait a minute, that's not how we saw it, Moses! You wouldn't believe the immense size of the fruit in that land. Look at these grapes; we had to carry this heavy cluster between two poles! The place is exactly as God promised -- a land filled with 'milk and honey.' There are, it is true, a race of giant people living in great walled-cities here and there, but they are no match for the God of Abraham. He has brought us this far; will He not complete what He has promised?"

God did complete what He had promised for Caleb and Joshua, but not for those who cowardly refused to enter the Promised Land. When the rest of the Israelites heard news of the spies' report they too turned their backs on the visible fruits of the Promised Land and chose to remain in the desert wilderness of Kadesh-Barnea. There they eventually died off. Those who shrank back in order to save their lives, lost their lives instead.

Their undoing painfully demonstrates, to all of us, and for all time, the dispensableness of an unfaithful generation -- even one previously chosen and led by God!

Years later Jesus said these words recorded in Mark 8:34-36: "If anyone wants to become my follower, let him deny himself and take up his cross and follow Me. For he who wants to save his life will lose it, and he who loses his life for My sake, and the sake of the Gospel, will save it." The point had already been proven by the Kadesh-Barnea Israelites in Canaan.

The main problem for God was not getting the Israelites out of Egypt; it was getting Egypt out of them! His problem continues today. It is easier to get a person out of worldly surroundings than it is to get worldliness out of the person.

Troubles and afflictions strengthen true faith but inevitably lead to the failure of superficial faith. Like the Children of Israel who turned back at the brink of the Promised Land, Christians today, get within range of their personal crosses and have second thoughts.

The Israelites, though they were accustomed to God delivering them from the worst of otherwise impossible circumstances, still wavered in their dedication and their superficial faith failed. Thus, they did not enter the land nor did they bring forth any fruit.

That is the reason our popular interpretation calls the thorny heart the "Kadesh-Barnea-Christian." The thorns represent afflictions and other problems that choke the seed, and if those thorns are allowed to prevail then the seed fails and does not bring forth fruit.

By the hand of God over one-million adults had crossed the Red Sea but only two became fit enough in their faith that they were permitted to enter the Promised Land. The people of Israel, with the exception of Caleb and Joshua, could not possibly bear fruit with their sterile faith so they were stayed by God in the wilderness until they died off.

By looking more closely at the thorns in the parable and at what they symbolize, perhaps we can come to a greater understanding of what produces a sterile faith that will not allow the bearing of fruit.

2. Read Mark 4:7 and then Mark 4:18,19. Name the three breeds of thorns (composites of human desires) that choke the growth of Christian character?

Thorn 1: THE CARES OF THE WORLD

3. Read Luke chapter 10 verse 38 - 41. Who invited Jesus to her home?

4. Who was making the preparations for His stay?

5. What was her sister doing?

6. What did Martha ask Jesus?

7. Do you think this was a fair question? Why or why not? Did Jesus indicate to Martha that her question was unessential? Explain.

"The cares of the world" can be described as an anxious unrelaxed focus on the business of present life which chokes the seed. Any number of interests, legitimate in their place, are allowed to dominate one's life, with Christian profession being no more than just another segment of an already highly segmented life. Preoccupied "Christians" permit spiritual convictions to come to nothing because of their habitual submission to petty distractions and less noble influences. All these fill their hearts with terminal anxieties. Such people, like Martha, "cumbered with much serving," miss the joy and privilege of sitting at Christ's feet.

Thorn 2: THE DECEITFULNESS OF RICHES

8. Read Mark 10:17-31.

When Jesus and His disciples are met by a rich young ruler, the disciples are amazed at Jesus' remarks. They are amazed simply because of the universal feeling, then as now, that the rich can get whatever they want. It was difficult for these ordinary workers (His disciples) to realize that God's standard for dealing with the rich is different from man's. What made this understanding even more difficult for the disciples to grasp was that it was commonly taught then that wealth was a sign of God's favor bestowed upon a person.

9. In Mark 10:23-26 the disciples are amazed at Jesus' remarks. Note especially verses 23 and 24; Jesus changes His emphasis in vs. 23 from rich to what emphasis in vs. 24?

10. Do you think He changed His emphasis in verses 23 and 24 to help His disciples understand something? If so, what?

11. Must a person be wealthy to place trust in financial security? Explain.

12. Look up the story of the Rich Fool in Luke 12:16-21. In verse 11, what do you think is meant by "true riches?"

13. How are the Pharisees described in verse 14?

14. How are they described in verse 15?

15. What does Psalm 49 say are the thoughts of those who are rich but have no understanding of God?

16. Compare the description of the rich who have no understanding in Psalms 49:10-20[1] to the Rich Fool in Luke 12:16-21.

17. Look up the prayer of Agur in Proverbs 30:8,9. Note Agur's awareness of his own limitations. Have You mastered this awareness in your own life? In what ways could you improve?

---

1. Ps. 49:12, 20 says "man in his pomp is like the beasts that perish." The comparison of pompous men to beasts implies that their level of *understanding* is equivalent to a beast who cannot reason about life or God's existence. Beasts have little, if any, reasoning capacity which is why they are often called "dumb" animals. Man in his pomp, without God, is no better off than a dumb animal.

It is impossible for man to save the rich or poor but God can and has saved both in all ages.

Money or wealth in itself is not wrong or sinful. It is the *love of money* or *worship* of it that is wrong. It is important to remember that you do not have to have money to love it or desire it too strongly. In other words, you don't have to have possessions or wealth in order to *lust* after it.

The material and financial blessings indirectly given through new life in Christ may become a curse. This happens when the blessings given take the place reserved for the Blessing Giver. Jesus refers to this as "the deceitfulness of riches." Our prayers should not be for blessings, but for hearts able to receive blessings without being turned away from the Source.

Thorn 3: THE LUST OF OTHER THINGS

Most Christians are sufficiently familiar with warnings against the *lust* of other things (*desire* is translated as *lust* in certain biblical versions).[1]

This phrase, 'the lust of other things,' may be interpreted as 'an indulgence in the pleasures of this life.' Enjoyments, innocent in moderation, in which one begins to over-indulge without restraint, soon begins to choke the seed. So much time is allotted for pleasure that only momentary snatches remain for spiritual things. In the early stages of Christian growth there appeared some "promise" of fruit, but other "desires" prevented the fruit from maturing, resulting in the neglect of the needs of the soul for eternity. Such was the case with the Rich young Ruler who wanted his possessions and God to hold equal place in his heart. This was not possible for one must be esteemed over the other. They cannot be held with equal priority because no man can serve two masters. Lust comes in many varieties: power, prestige, popularity, position, reputation, etc. Examples of sexual lust and other appetites are also rampant.

One of the many sad effects of the emphasis on sex at every turn in our society is that an entire generation has

1. The same Greek word is used for lust and desire. In English means *desire* when used in a legitimate context, *lust* when used in an illegal or bad sense. In Greek the context determines the semantic value.

been robbed of the true definition of *love* by equating its meaning to feelings and sexual acts alone.

17. What does the world point to as the greatest act of love today?

18. In Ephesians 5:31, 32, what is the great mystery that is symbolic of the relationship between Christ and the Church? Do we normally think of this relationship when we think of this act? Discuss why it is no longer natural for Christians to equate these two things.

19. What does Jesus say the greatest act of love is in John 15:13? Who has done this for you?

20. List some of the attributes of love described by Paul in I Corinthians 13.

21. In light of these verses how can you show *real* love to others?

22. How can you show your love to God (I John 5:3)?

Because many people today think of sex when they think of love does that mean it is normal to equate these two? A good question--what is normal. Is it typical, or average, or usual, or natural? Just what is the meaning of "normal?"

WHAT IS NORMAL?

Imagine a deadly plague striking our world and spreading rapidly, killing people by the thousands with no cure in sight. Within only a few short years the average human life span drops from seventy-two years of age to thirty-five.

Supposing the crisis continues unhindered, it would not be long before thirty-five would be considered the "normal" or "average" human life span. Eventually even the plague itself might be considered "normal" but that would not make it, or death at 35, natural, -- only "normal" in the sense of "usual" or "typical."

We must be cautious not to view what is "usual" or "typical" in society as normal or as a standard for measuring our behavior.

This is exactly what took place during the terrible events of the holocaust. Hitler himself said that if something is repeated often enough the people will believe it. And Hitler and others before him repeated their ideologies so long and so emphatically that the hideousness of the results became lost for a time in the shadows of evil doctrine.

The imprisoned Jewish people were not visible to the public and the continued hype that they were a sub- standard race became believable through the repetitive rhetoric of political leaders and politically controlled media. Even in the prison camps the people were clothed uniformly with only numbers for names so that the guards began to view them as sub-human and disposable. Being starved and mistreated beyond all appearance of healthy human beings only made it easier to treat them as "sub-human and disposable."

Often it is asked how humanity could allow such a terrible massacre to take place, yet the inquirer may neglect to see the similarity in the 30 million and rising number of abortions which continue largely because of the same lies and method -- the fetus is sub-human; it doesn't even look fully human and the public doesn't see and is not aware of the horror as the fetus remains imprisoned and butchered in the womb of a gender known for nurturing; and at the hand of a profession known for dignity and respect for life.

We must be extremely careful to view reality through God's Word, and not the temporary always shifting paradigms of our culture and environment.

The next set of exercises may seem exaggerated in accord with everyday living, because most of the "lusts" we will be discussing appear so "normal" and harmless in our world, and our churches. Nevertheless, when unrestrained, and out of control they become lethal "thorns" stemming from the "cares of the world; the deceitfulness of riches; and the lust of other things."

24. Describe ways that things such as money, food, sex etc., which are not inherently bad can become evil forces in our lives.

We have noted that many lusts stem from a desire to gratify one or more of the five senses, but lust is not always tangible; it can take on as many forms as there are desires of the heart, mind and soul. Lust is simply an inordinate or illegal use of something intended as good when kept within its legitimate design and context. It becomes excessive when it supersedes our love for the Lord, our fellow man, or even ourselves.

The turning point from desire to lust is when desire supersedes its healthy and proper limits. At this point, "lust is conceived"and "gives birth to sin."

25. Match the following scriptures to the examples below shown in the opposite column by placing the correct scripture in the blank in this column opposite the example. Note the examples this time do not correspond to the 5 senses. They are intangible and more difficult to discern, but they are still examples of activities that, though good and reasonable within their proper limitations, turn to destructive "lusts" when not kept within their proper bounds.

Matthew 10:37.
James 3:14 -16.
Exodus 20:12.
Matthew 20:20-28.
James 4:11,12

Lust of learning: too strong of a desire for higher education, or a "lettered education."

"Lust for power and/or significance":
Ambition out of control -- too strong of a desire for a title, role, position or recognition. This kind of lust is not limited to the workplace or politics. The lust for power is found in social clubs, the class-room, even the church.

Lust for power and/or significance (via gossip): having the latest, often most damaging information whether good or bad, true or untrue, can afford one great power and prestige. But gossips are not alone in their lust, those who listen are accomplices feeding their own lusts for having the inside story even if they do not repeat it.

Jesus was aware of the damage gossip can cause especially when put forth by respected members of the community, for it was the Pharisees who were saying he was a drunkard and a glutton, and a friend to tax gatherers and prostitutes.

Lust over loved-ones: Parents who dote over their children unnaturally beyond the age of childhood into their adult years. By making idols of their children or overprotecting them they handicap them socially and otherwise. Everyone has seen mothers who suffocate their adult children in seemingly harmless, yet damaging ways in order to satisfy their own selfishness by not letting go of their child. The dedication that leads parents to do so well when children are small can also lead them to hold on too tightly when they are grown.[1] This is because the parents have turned their focus of original love and commitment for their children in toward themselves.

The same kind of self-focused love extended toward another can sometimes be seen between spouses too.

Lust for security: the reverse is true of children who will not leave the nest. A fear of independence and unnaturally prolonged desire to nestle securely under their parents' wings is really inverted selfishness.

26. Have you noticed evidence in yourself or others of any lusts we have mentioned so far? If you have noticed something in another, you should pray for his enlightenment. If you have noticed it in yourself, what will your course of action be for correcting it?

27. Do you think lust could be the same as idol-worship? Look up Exodus 20:3-6. What does it mean "you shall not make for yourself an idol?" Does this simply mean fashioning an image, or does "make for yourself" possibly mean more? Explain.

28. Look up Colossians 3:1-10. What is referred to as "idolatry?"

Idolaters are not just people who worship a golden calf or statue. An idolater is one who puts any interest[1] above his or her interest in God.

If you are more interested in golf than God, then golf is your idol. If you have more interest in: shopping, cooking, cleaning, education, career, money, health, sickness, sports, hobbies, TV, politics, computers, friends, children, spouse, or grandchildren; or, even more interest in your own ministry or spiritual gifts, than you have in God, then that is your idol. You are an idolater!

How can you determine whether or not you are an idolater? When you have a free moment during the day, what do you routinely think about? When you are not

1. *Any interest* is used here in the context of covetousness because, in essence, any interest which claims more free time, attention, and devotion than God and His interests is a covetous interest, which is idolatry. To covet means to set one's heart upon, 'to pant after.'

concentrating on daily responsibilities at home or work, what do you routinely day dream about? What do your thoughts routinely return to when they are not occupied by regular responsibilities? Chances are this is your idol, or potential idol, if your answer was not God and the things pertaining to His kingdom. (MT 6:33).

Now that you know how the sin of idol worship manifests itself, you can guard against it. Use the process described above to examine yourself periodically to see if you are in the faith (2 Cor. 13:5).

It is important to realize that an idol is not necessarily something enjoyable. An idol can just as easily be something or someone you despise or are afraid of. Many pagans worship the things they are most afraid of such as snakes or poisonous insects. The same application can be made to us when our thoughts continually return to something we are afraid of, or to someone who has hurt or injured us in some way we cannot forgive. We become enslaved to these thoughts until they become our master--our idol.

A person's interests, support, devotion and the way she spends her time represent what is most valuable to her. A person may claim to be a Christian but live and practice something entirely different than he claims. One can be so acceptable to the world that she is not acceptable to God.

The way one lives is not necessarily the same as what one "claims to believe." We must be careful not to fool ourselves--each of us lives according to what we really believe.

The proof of what one *really* believes is found in a person's lifestyle. Even though he may claim a particular belief or religion, if he does not live according to his claim, he does not really have faith or belief in it at all. Remember the meaning of *believe* in the original language of the Bible means "to live in accordance with." In this respect, many who call themselves Christian must realize they are not genuine Christians at all but simply "Christian-sympathizers." They prefer, or sympathize, with the case for Christianity, but they do not live in accordance with what they prefer.

In summary, God alone deserves and can bear our supreme affection (Exodus 20:3). Once anything takes primary preoccupation over and above Christ, its value drops to the level of filthy rags whether it is "normal" or "successful" in everyday life or not. Then, and only then, do the "normal" and "successful" things of everyday life become thorns that choke the Word, make it unfruitful, and damn the soul.

The "passing away of old things and the arrival of new" occurs primarily in the sense of "new life," but also in multiple secondary ways. Usually, new Christians begin attending Church; some also attend mid-week services, and small prayer groups or Bible studies during the week. But most importantly, new Christians experience an observable shift for the better in their attitude and love towards God and others. There is a tendency to be more honest, industrious, helpful and kind. Eventually, this upwards-shift in overall character begins to reap some blessings as the result of the behavior change. Hence the Christian, who is now more mature and pure in Christ, begins to prosper, and depending on his preference many things can happen.

But how do thorns take root in the hearts of truly settled believers in Christ?

The following story illustrates much of what we are talking about regarding "thorny soil." First answer question 29, then read the story carefully and answer the questions at the end. Be prepared to discuss your answers.

29. Look up 2 Corinthians 5:17. What happens when one becomes a Christian?

<u>BLESSING OR CURSE</u>?

Joe Landon had just turned 35; he had a wife and two kids; his friendly relaxed manner made him well-liked among co-workers and neighbors; and he was a part of the "up and coming" management team at his office. Joe didn't take in a lot of recreational activities outside of the community water ski club he had started three years ago. Otherwise Joe spent most of his time with his family, played poker with buddies on Wednesday night, and caught Monday night football without fail.

He had always been considered a "pretty good guy" and though he would never admit to it, Joe thought of himself that way too. After all, he had been a good husband, father, and provider for his family; he'd been a dependable worker and loyal friend; and he'd never been in much trouble outside of his days of fraternity college pranks. He had no strong vices, just a few beers during poker games and Monday night football.

Joe, no doubt, had been careful to take good care of himself and his little family, he was sure of that, up until a few weeks ago.

The Goodwins were new to the area and were moving into the house next to Joe's on the east. The driveways of the homes were side by side so the Landons and the Goodwins had seen one another as they were coming and going during the day, though they had not formally met. That evening, both families pulled into their drive at the same time and seeing the opportunity was prime, Joe leapt from his car to make the first introduction.

He barely got the words "Hello, I'm Joe" from his mouth as his new neighbor grasped his outstretched hand with a tight but comfortable shake saying, "Clint Goodwin here, nice to meet ya."

The two men hit it off immediately and through the course of their small-talk, Joe learned that Clint was the new pastor at the church just around the corner near the end of the block. The sun was dipping below the roof tops and the air was starting to nip so both men expressed their pleasure at meeting and turned for their open garages, but not before Clint Goodwin invited Joe's family to visit his new church on Sunday.

As Joe entered the house he called to his wife, "Honey, the new guy next door seems great, and can you guess what he does for a living?"

Without waiting for a reply Joe hollered, "He's a pastor!" As he walked into the kitchen he found his wife, Judy, making dinner. Joe helped set the table as he told her that Clint had invited them to church on Sunday. Joe and Judy weren't churchgoers but they agreed they would attend.

"After all," Judy said, "it might be kind of interesting and it would be good experience for the kids."

Both Joe and Judy felt an obligation to show this courtesy to their new neighbors; it was a small price to pay for getting along in the future.

Next Sunday, to the Landons' surprise they found Clint's sermon very intriguing, even more than they had politely expressed to him afterwards. The Landons showed up next week and the week thereafter and Joe started spending time at Clint's after work on week nights.

About 8 weeks later, Joe was sitting alone in the den thinking over the whole series of events--he had decided to give his life to Christ.

"It seems ironic," thought Joe releasing a faint chuckle under his breath, "I always thought of myself *as a Christian.* I grew up in America and I was a pretty good guy -- honest, and have never been in much trouble."

But in the last weeks Joe had gained some insight. Though he had never considered God much, Joe thought he had lived his life as best he could. Now it looked different, he could see how small and self-focused it had been to live for the happiness and welfare of himself and his little family alone. True, he had worked hard and been a good neighbor, but it was mostly for selfish reasons--he could see that now.

Most of Joe's kindness had been based on the idea that if you're nice then people will be nice to you, and though his motto had proved true, it was motivated by selfish regard for himself and his family. Sure, he had helped John McCormick with his new fence and Jill Hollister put on new snow tires but in the back of his mind he knew they would tell everyone what a great guy he was and that was far better than having them say he was lazy, un-friendly, or worse yet --selfish.

That was the ironic part, selfishness, not love, had been the motive behind Joe's good-guy nature all of his life; he just hadn't realized it before. Now it seemed so pale and flimsy in the light of real love--God's love. Joe saw that if he did not love God supremely he would never be able to love his neighbors as he loved himself and his family. That is why he had decided to become a Chris-tian; he knew that the only way he could quit loving him-self and his family supremely was to repent of his selfishness and turn to Christ for forgiveness. Then, once restored to a right relationship with God, he could begin to restore a right relationship with his family and friends--loving God supremely and others as himself.

Joe had been a good guy by most standards yet the change that Christ made in his life was phenomenal. He dropped Monday night football and began going on visitation with Clint; Joe loved to tell his friends about his new under-standing of true love and how it resulted in new life in Christ. He canceled his Wednesday night poker game and invited his pals to Bible study at Clint's. Most of Joe's buddies never showed, but others came and the study thrived. And, it was no longer a chore to help his co-workers and neighbors, but a pleasure and welcome opportunity to show Christ's love for them.

Seven months later, Joe was returning to his office after lunch and as he entered the reception area, the secretary handed him a note saying that Mr. McCormick, the CEO, wanted to see Joe in his office right away.

Nervously Joe checked his look in the reception room mirror, cinched the knot in his tie, then headed down the long corridor to the CEO's office. The door was open so Joe poked his head around the corner.

Mr. McCormick looked up from his desk and said, "Come in Joe, close the door and have a seat, I need to discuss a few things with you."

His mind racing in search for a clue as to the purpose of this meeting, Joe sank in the nearer of two leather, wing-back chairs.

Joe's thoughts were cut-short by McCormick's words, "Joe, I've noticed some changes in you over the last few months; your reports are consistently ahead of schedule, well-researched, and organized."

Joe felt a surge of relief that soon vanished as quickly as it had come.

"That's not all," said McCormick in a piercing tone, "you seemed to have rid yourself of a few annoying habits. At our Monday business meetings you no longer try to make yourself look good by coyly mentioning the faults of others and then laying claim to their good work. You may have thought you were being shrewd but I saw through it. Whatever your reason, I'm glad you've wised-up.

Furthermore, I've noticed your average monthly expenses have dropped significantly."

Joe felt a twinge of shame rush through him as the heat of his guilt highlighted his neck and ears in a rosy pink. All the staff fudged a little on their expense reports -- it was just part of the business world. Now that Joe had quit padding his expenses, he found he was caught; his new honesty had implicated him. Joe expected a hand-slap stronger than at first but surprisingly did not receive it."Joe, I know most employees cheat a great deal on their expense reports; it's so common nowadays I've come to expect it. We even make allowances for it in our annual budget! It's a damn shame too... "

Joe grimaced slightly but Mr. McCormick didn't notice. Joe was relieved that he hadn't and that he kept on talking.

"I sure don't approve of this white collar crime but I haven't found a way to stop it. Anyway, Joe, the heart of the matter is, I haven't seen expense reports as low as yours since the early sixties!"

Joe inhaled as he opened his mouth to respond but was again cut short.

"That's not all, Joe. You've been employed here for 8 years now but in the last 7 months you've produced twice as much as you ever have annually. Joe, I want to reward this new attitude and productiveness you've shown. Because your honesty, integrity, consideration and diligence have excelled beyond measure you are being promoted to Vice President of Operations and will receive a $10,000 raise and $5,000 annual bonus plus the benefits that go with your new position.

Joe was stunned. He knew it was nothing short of a blessing from God. Joe thanked his CEO and as they stood vigorously shaking hands across the desk, Joe offered to explain how all of these changes in his character took place. McCormick buzzed his secretary and had her schedule lunch for the two of them next week.

Joe left the office that day bristling with joy not only at his new promotion but his chance to share Christ with the CEO next week over lunch. He couldn't wait to tell everyone and ask them to pray for him.

More months passed, along with Thanksgiving, Christmas and New Year's. It was now mid February and Joe found himself lapsing into daydreams of Springtime and water skiing. With his recent job promotion Joe could easily afford a ski boat and new equipment.

"Why not," he mused, "the Lord knows I love to ski, and He wants us to enjoy an abundant life. Besides, I gave up the ski club for church activities; God won't mind; in fact, I'm sure this is just another way He wants to bless us."

As the weather warmed, Joe's family could be found at the lake every Saturday until fall arrived.

Joe had such a great time back on his skis that when next Spring arrived and school was out he talked with Judy and they decided to spend Saturdays and Sundays at the lake. This meant that Judy would have to find someone to substitute teach her 3rd grade Sunday School Class; that was the only hitch, but a solvable one.

Joe and Judy remained active in their Wednesday night Bible study and everyone seemed happy for them. Sometimes Pastor Goodwin and his family joined them on their boat on Saturdays.

Fall and winter came and left again without much incident except that Joe's company instituted a new benefit for top executives who kept to their budget and exceeded their goals -- a 4-day work week! Those who met the conditions could choose between Fridays or Mondays off. Joe took Monday.

Now he could spend 3-day weekends at the lake. With this thought, he snatched up his phone and dialed the number of the resort on the lake.

As the phone rang Joe was thinking, "This will be great, no more hassle driving to and from the lake every day. Lord, please let at least one cabin be left."

The person on the end of the line said one cabin was left and without a pause Joe reeled off his credit card number to cover the deposit. He could hardly believe he was able to secure a cabin; this late in the year they were usually booked up.

"It must have been the Lord, again," Joe thought and smiled.

It wasn't until days later that it occurred to Joe he would have to discontinue Monday visitation with Clint while he was at the lake.

"Oh well," he reasoned, "there are so many new Christians in our church, it's time they did some of the work. It would be good experience for them." Joe felt he had served his time and paid his dues, he was an elder now and didn't require the fundamental activities.

Summer arrived and the cabin was perfect except it was a bit far from the lake but Joe thought the drive wasn't bad compared to going all the way home and back. The family had plenty of free time, so much in fact that the evenings especially dragged on until they met new friends.

Joe's new pals usually played poker in the evening while the wives talked and the kids played. Joe couldn't wait to join in the game, he thought it would be a good chance to witness and because he wanted to be liked, Joe took the beer the guys offered him.

Most of the Landons' new friends were retired and lived at the lake year round. Joe and Judy grew so attached to them that they were sad about parting for the winter. So Joe decided to extend their lease through the fall. This way he could play poker and catch Monday night football with his pals before heading home late at night. They would keep two cars at the lake and Judy and the kids could drive home Sunday night so the kids could make it to school on Monday.

Whether he wanted to admit it or not, Joe's lake life was starting to take a toll on him and it was showing on Tuesday mornings. He was often late and though well-dressed he had a bedraggled look. Joe was unalert most of the day and virtually listless after lunch; once the receptionist had heard him snoring over her intercom at 2:30 in the afternoon. To make matters worse Joe was falling behind in his work load.

Enough was enough. He knew he had to do something before he lost his 4-day work-week privilege. Joe decided he had no alternative. He would give up Wednesday night Bible Studies until he caught up, but not before asking the group to pray for him, that he might not lose his new benefits.

During the next weeks while Joe was struggling to meet deadlines, Mr. McCormick was reconsidering his 4-day-work-week program. For a couple of his employees it was working beautifully but for the rest it was sheer disaster.

Ken Phillips was clearly a golf addict, though it hadn't effected his work or anyone else's too much. But now that he had more time for tournaments, he was driving the rest of the staff nuts showing them pictures and telling tales. His constant boasting distracted everyone.

Jeff Sumpter, who had been an avid social drinker and reported to make quite a fool of himself, was now a premier alcoholic. Not showing up for days and never calling in after his binges was about to cost him his job; he had already lost his 4-day week privilege but it appeared there was no turning back.

Gary Alberts now found time to play the "nothing down" real estate purchasing game. His newly acquired properties came with newly acquired tenant problems that were distracting him from work and tempting him with a nervous breakdown.

Chief Accountant, Karen Stewart, had suffered with bouts of mild depression for years but with the extra time a 4 day work-week allowed Karen's symptoms evolved into a chronic sleeping disorder. She was now seeing a psychiatrist at $200 an hour on company insurance and time. This wasn't what bothered Mr. McCormick, he was glad to help any way he could. It was the fact that Karen had been better off working 5 days per week and that her new "benefit," a 4-day work week, had proved harmful for her. McCormick felt responsible.

Only Bert Schmidt and Suzanne Canfield seemed to be prospering through the new program. Both were professing Christians and they spent their long weekend in extra family time and helping the sick and poor. Plus Bert helped his pastor on Mondays and Suzanne led a prayer group on Friday mornings.

Then there was Joe Landon, he was McCormick's favorite because it was Joe who had first introduced McCormick to Christ over lunch 3 years ago. McCormick fondly recalled that day.

Preston McCormick was not one to make hasty decisions, he had not achieved success as CEO by doing that. So McCormick didn't swallow the whole of Christianity along with his lunch. But Christ had his attention and McCormick wouldn't be satisfied until he'd made a thorough investigation of Christianity. Even then, it was not until he saw how his own life without Christ fell short that McCormick fully embraced Christianity and Jesus became his purpose for living.

It was this new purpose in life, that motivated McCormick to initiate the 4-day week program. He wanted to thank his employees for their loyalty and hard work. Over the years they had received enough raises to be more than satisfied financially, so he thought a 4 day week would be just the incentive to reward and inspire them.

McCormick's new Life in Christ had blossomed with a new generosity that could be traced back to lunch that day with Joe Landon. That's why he had such a soft spot for Joe even though he had been consistently disappointed with him over the last few years.

Landon's life and work had glistened compared to the rest at first but his passion for water skiing had gradually taken over until only the dross was left of his original dedication to Jesus. The sad thing was everyone seemed to recognize it but Joe. He was too preoccupied trying to catch up on his work load and maintain his recreational lifestyle.

McCormick was determined to keep praying for Joe that he would listen to the Holy Spirit convicting him once more of sin and righteousness but he knew it was up to Joe to pause and listen to the voice of God -- it would be difficult to hear over the wake of his water-skis, and the tumult of his work load.

The blessings afforded to Joe by his new life as a Christian began to gnaw away at his foundational relationship with Christ until the blessings became a curse because they weakened that relationship and threatened to smother it. This is what is meant by *the deceitfulness of riches; the lust of other things; and the cares of life* -- known as *thorns.*

It is clear from our story that certain consequences follow certain actions. Every choice a person makes has primary, secondary, and often further consequences that impact his life and the lives of others.

30. **List as many good or bad consequences as you can think of that were related to Joe receiving a job promotion.**

31. **What determined whether the consequences were good or bad?**

32. **List as many good or bad consequences as you can that resulted from Mr. McCormick's institution of a 4-day-work-week.**

33. **What determined whether the 4-day-work-week consequences turned good or bad?**

If the extra day-off from work had been *routinely* used to serve the Lord, help the sick, elderly and others; study God's Word, pray for friends, family, countries and their leaders, and countless other beneficial ways of loving our neighbors as ourselves, it would undoubtedly have been a blessing.

Conversely, if the extra day was *routinely* spent in a frenzy of self-indulgent recreations such as watching TV, sleeping, over-eating, getting drunk, camping, water-skiing, golfing, carousing, pursuing get-rich-ventures, or indulging the flesh and feeding selfishness in any other measure, it would surely prove to be a curse.

This is not to say that the extra day should not *occasionally* have been used for recreation or rest, but only that when *routinely* used this way, no matter how harmless the activity, it would eventually become a curse through the process of dissipation that results naturally as the consequence of selfish pursuit.

On the bright side, those who choose to live intelligently, making wise, morally-correct choices spent in *routinely* wise and intelligent activity generate good consequences--rewards, which are pleasant, productive, and beneficial in contrast with wrong choices--that reap low, painful, often destructive results.

The age-old process described here is known as natural law. There are consequences inseparably connected to choices. Those consequences are either negative or positive depending on the choice.

34. What is the "pivot point" that determines whether consequences are good and rewarding or painful and punitive?

35. Look up John 15:4. When we allow our affections to shift from the Source to the blessing are we abiding in Christ? Explain.

36. If one is abiding among thorns can she bear fruit? Explain.

Often only a fine line between blessings and idols exists in one's heart. Frequently, the emphasis cannot be distinguished except by revelation of the Holy Spirit. This is because true blessings (before they turn into curses) are good when maintained in proper context. It is the unnoticed shift in the heart that brings about the change from positive to negative.

Many professing Christians have either sunk to or never risen above the level of atheists or agnostics -- people who conduct their lives as if there were no God. The pressured tempo of self-centered living has crowded out the time God would use to mentor them in the ways of the Spirit. "Here is no lack of soil, perhaps good soil; but what is deficient is a careful husbandry, the extermination of thorns and weeds. The profession of spiritual life is retained, but the power of religion is by degrees eaten out."[1]

When a person realizes that the condition of his or her spiritual life is one of profession without power there are only two alternatives. One, he may have a change of heart (Ezekiel 18:31) and begin to live up to the Biblical standard for one's life. Or, he must try to dilute the Biblical standard to fit his current lifestyle and continue living a deceived life.

37. **Read 2 Tim. 3:5-8. How does this passage describe the kind of people whose hearts are symbolized by thorny soil?**

Everyone has seen plants that have withered and died from weeds and thorns choking them. This is precisely what happens to a Christian's growth when the cares of the world, the lure of wealth, and the desire for other things, take primary occupation of his time, energy, and resources. The result for the plant is that it produces no fruit (Mark 4:7). The parallel in the professing Christian, choked by the cares of the world, the deceitfulness of riches and the lust of other things, is also no fruit.

Nowhere, does the Bible conclude that the divided heart has no religion, only that it is a stunted, unstable and false religion (James 1:1-8). When God's promises and the world's promises are considered equally good, there will be an attempt made to serve God and Mammon. The cares of the world and its pleasures are the thorny briars and brambles that strangle the life of one's soul.

Thus, when planted on thorny soil the seed takes root but bears no fruit. It is choked and symbolizes preoccupied people. The truth takes hold, but that hold is gradually loosened by a trio of thorns. Preoccupations in opposition to or competition with the nature of the seed are permitted ground.

---

1. R. C. Trench, *Notes on Parables of Our Lord,* (Grand Rapids, Michigan, Baker Book House, 1980), p. 31.

The deadly poison of the thorns is based on the world's greatest lie, that is, a person must live primarily for his or her own happiness. Thus, the thorny heart continues in selfishness, all the while believing he or she is on the way to heaven.

The idea that to be happy one must live primarily in the pursuit of personal happiness is absolutely false. Real joy, peace, and contentment always elude anyone who tries to be happy this way. Genuine happiness can never be attained as an end in itself, it can only be embraced as a by-product, the by-product that stems from loving God supremely and others as oneself.

38. Is there such a thing as optional or partial discipleship? Why or why not?

Section II: The Responsibility of The Sower Who Sows on Thorny Ground

The sower's first priority is to pray. Pray for awakening conviction brought by the Holy Spirit to open the eyes of the one whose heart is overgrown by thorns. The sower's second priority is to pray again but to pray for opportunities to gently and lovingly confront the person with the their condition of heart and their need for change. One word of caution should be considered and that is that no sower is equipped to take on the delicate task of confronting another unless that sower is sure his own heart is free and clear of stones and thorns.

The earlier comparison of "thorny soil" to the wandering children of Israel who finally reached the border of the promised land but refused to enter and chose to remain in Kadesh-Barnea is clearly accurate. One cannot be truly Christian and "Kadesh-Barnea- natured" or growing on "thorny ground" simultaneously. This is a seriously neglected problem in our churches -- the Kadesh-Barnea-product of thorny ground.

But let's look at how a sower should respond to the thorns outside of The Church.

1. Look up Ezekiel 33:1-20. To whom is the watchman (the sower) to give warning.

2. Who will be held responsible for the death of the wicked person who has not been warned by the watchman (the sower). (List two responsible parties.)

1)
2)

3. Who is responsible for the death of the wicked person who has been warned.

The unprecedented gift of salvation carries with it an added responsibility: every person who receives this gift is held accountable not only for her own soul, but is charged with the responsibility of caring for the souls around her. To every sower, meaning to every Christian, God says, "I have set you as a watchman... therefore hear the word at my mouth, and give them warning from me."

We briefly covered the proper manner of confronting those with "thorny hearts" in the first paragraph of this section. But unfortunately this approach is the least common one observed among church members.

Because the problem of thorny hearts exists inside the church and not just outside her doors, the easiest course for the sower is to ignore their existence hoping the problem will somehow correct itself. This most common response is by far the most negligent.

4. Again, what will be the consequences for the sower who ignores the existence of "thorny hearts" and does nothing to warn Them?

6

Sowing On Good Soil

The fourth and final soil is the good and fertile ground which consistently yields a bountiful harvest of thirty, sixty, even one hundred percent return on the seed sown.

1. Review the symbols in this parable which we have discussed so far. Tell what each symbol represents in the space provided after that symbol in the opposite column.

Seed

Sower

Path

Stony Ground

Thorny Ground *(List the three types of thorns and what they represent)*

Good Ground

Harvest/Fruit

Fruit results when the Word is sown accurately on the fertile soil of receptive hearts. Luke 8:15 says, "But that on the good ground are they, which, in an honest and good heart, having heard the word, keep it, and bring forth fruit. It is important to understand that only the good soil corresponds to a good heart. The varying descriptions in the Gospel accounts, "Being of the truth," "doing truth," "the soil of a good and honest heart," all mean a love for God and a willingness to live a life pleasing to Him.

Those whose hearts symbolically consist of good ground are not 'half-hearted' or lackadaisical, they understand what it means to love God with all their heart (supreme motivation) and to be busy about serving Him.

Good soil can best be described as one with the heart to pay attention, and understand, taking some time away from work or a daily routine to have more time in prayer and study. This one follows through on what was heard and becomes obedient to all she is aware to be right and true. This person's consecration in lifestyle matches her comprehension.

So we see that real Christians not only *ought* to love God with all their heart,--THEY DO!

What does loving God with a whole heart mean? It is not simply declaring a preference for God without equivalent consecration in one's lifestyle. A person's life always, without exception, corresponds to what that person truly believes. This is, sadly, not always the same as what he prefers or claims to believe.

Persons who advocate Christianity without consistent evidence of it in their lifestyle are those whose hearts are stony and thorny ground. These affirm the truth of Christianity, that Jesus is their Savior, but they live their lives otherwise--consumed by the attractions and fears that represent those who belong to the world, not Christ.

These are "Christian-sympathizers," meaning they sympathize with, or they prefer, the teachings of Christianity and they may honestly believe themselves to be Christian but their lifestyle betrays them, proving their lack of what it takes to be a genuine Christian.

Christian-sympathizers have a state of mind not stubbornly repelling truth, but lacking in earnestness; the same spirit which was in the minds of the great multitudes who followed Jesus, to whom he turned and told in the strongest language what discipleship to him involved (Luke 14:25-33). It is the same mind-set which was in the Children of Israel who neglected to cross the border at Kadesh-Barnea into the Promised Land. This frame of mind is no doubt enlightened to the Truth but has not yet acted upon it, it has not crossed the border from Kadesh-Barnea into the "promised land" of genuine salvation.

2. Look up Luke 14: 25 - 33. What does discipleship to Jesus involve?

3. Look up Luke 14:26. List those whom we are to love as ourselves but less than God.

Loving God with all your heart means that Jesus' goals are your priority and it shows in your life. If necessary, you will die for that Priority.

To love God, is to trust Christ. The basis of this trust is giving Him the supreme place in your affections and thus having the Gospel made a living reality in you. This must be done wholeheartedly. The evidence of wholeheartedness is serving and obeying Him. To believe on Him is to live in accordance with Him. This is the very essence and substance of a right relationship with God!

The Bible teaches that unless our supreme motive is right, no decisions, actions, or deeds of a secondary nature are worth any value.

It is important that we make no mistake: when we "ask Jesus into our heart," what we are really asking is that He take supreme place in our purpose --our entire reason for living and dying.

4. Look up Mark 4:20. How can you tell what kind of soil your heart is made of? Read Luke 8:11-15. Find the indicator as to whether or not a person's heart is made of good and fertile soil.

A heart which consists of good and fertile soil is not like the thorny and stony ground where the Gospel is a necessary imposition, an appendage attached lamely to a life of active selfishness. True Christianity is not an experience existing separately from other life experiences--it is the transformation of the whole life experience. Such transformation can only occur with a whole-hearted change, never a half-hearted-sentimental-preference for the Christian Faith.

The word of God insists on unswerving dedication from all who call themselves by His Name. The reason for such insistence is often misunderstood to mean that God is hard, strict, and unbending. This is far from true.

The truth is that God loves you, and in His gentle caring love, desires the very best for you. Therefore, because a life of loving God with all your heart is the very best thing for you, God requires it of you--because it is best for *you*! This is God's desire for you--that which is best for you--and this is evidence of His supreme love for you.

But God is too loving to force us to love Him, plus He knows that forced love is not genuine. He wants genuine love from us--so He leaves us the choice.

When we do not love God supremely, we inevitably, without exception, love ourselves, or something else supremely. Nothing and no one can withstand the weight of our supreme love except God, and He is the only One worth loving supremely. A supreme love for anything other than God will only serve to break our hearts and destroy our souls.

God desires the best for us and so He requires us to love Him with all our hearts and our fellow man as ourselves (not more or less). This is the highest and best good for all mankind.

Those whose hearts are symbolized in the parable by good soil are the only real Christians-- the ones who produce fruit! The only fruit-bearers of the four soils are those planted in good soil, these are the only ones with a secure hope for eternity.

The universal test to determine whether the motive of your heart is right, that is, whether the Word of God planted in your heart is in good and fertile soil, is whether that Word is fruitful (Mark 4:20).

Section 2: The Responsibility of the Sower Who Sows on Good Soil

The Responsibility of the Sower sowing on good soil is so simple it is often overlooked. Yet clearly there is a responsibility or there would not be noted different percentages of fruit harvested by the different sowers.

The soil, we are told, is good soil, therefore the difference in percentage of fruit harvested cannot be blamed on the condition of soil. The difference in the harvest must be blamed on the sower. Even on the best soil, a harvest will not take place if the sower does not sow.

The seed bears fruit only as it possesses the soil of an honest and good heart! (Luke 8:15). But what is meant by *fruit*? It is important that we know exactly because it is fruit that indicates one's wholehearted love for God.

5. In your own words explain the responsibility of the sower sowing on good soil. Make sure to explain the condition of soil as it relates to the conditions of men's hearts.

7
Fruit

Imagine we are playing a Bible-Words-Association Game. A white flash card is held up with the word **FRUIT** printed in bold black letters. You are to reply with the first thing that comes to your mind regarding *fruit* in a *Biblical context.*

1. What answer would you give? Circle your answer (a), (b), (c) or (d).

a) the *fruit* of the Spirit
b) figs
c) the "apple" Adam and Eve ate from the tree of knowledge of good and evil.
d) other (fill in your answer)

____

If you guessed any of the above answers, your answer would be correct. But when we look at all of these answers it is obvious they are not inter-changeable in their meanings though they are all *fruit.* Each has a very different meaning and context within the Bible.

Illustrations comparing men to plants and their work to fruits abound throughout the Old and New Testaments. The illustrations take on many forms from trees to vines to entire crops and they take on different figurative meanings as well. We are interested in the figurative meaning of fruit in the parable of the sower because the figurative meaning is the spiritual meaning.

We know when Jesus spoke of "fruit" in this parable He intended it literally in the story-line but He expected the figurative interpretation to transcend the literal into a spiritual application for those who were really listening.

Earlier, we covered the transition from the literal to the figurative, (or the earthly to the spiritual), by noting that the seed represents the Word, the sower represents Christians, and the soils represent hearers' hearts.

With all these clues it may seem simple to guess the spiritual meaning of fruit in this parable and most of us would guess correctly, but not totally. Most of our guesses would be only half right.

To fully realize what Jesus intended when He spoke of fruit in the Parable of the Sower we should define the literal meaning of fruit before we try to determine its spiritual context.

Following is the definition of "fruit" taken from Webster's Dictionary.

2. As you read through Webster's definition, fill in the blank spaces in each sample phrase with the word "fruit."

fruit *noun*

la: a product of plant growth (as grain, vegetables, or cotton)

[the ______________________(s) of the field]

b(l): The usually edible reproductive body of a seed plant; *esp:* one having a sweet pulp associated with the seed

[the ______________________ of the tree]

b(2): a succulent plant part used chiefly in a dessert or sweet course

c: a dish, quantity, or diet of fruits

[please pass the ______________]

d:a product of fertilization in a plant with its modified envelopes or appendages; *specif:* the ripened ovary of a seed plant and its contents

2 :OFFSPRING, PROGENY

3a: the state of bearing fruit [a tree in ______________]

b: the effect or consequence of an action or operation: **PRODUCT, RESULT**

[the ______________________(s) of his labor] [His work bore ______________________]

fruit•ed*adjective*, [2]**fruit** *verb intransitive:* **to bear fruit: to cause to bear fruit.**

3. Read through the definition above again and determine which segments apply to "fruit" as it is used in the context of the parable of the sower. Circle the ones which apply to the parable and cross out the ones which do not. Example:

Ia - would *literally* apply to **fruit** in the context of the parable of the Sower because it involves harvesting grain, the **fruit** of the field.

Ib(2) - would <u>not</u> apply to the Parable of the Sower because Jesus was not referring to the **part of fruit** used only in dessert dishes. When He told this parable He was talking about more than *a part of fruit* and something other than fruits which can be used in desserts.

4. Now that you have completed the above exercises, what do you think is the figurative (spiritual) meaning of fruit in the parable of the sower? What does "fruit" symbolize?

Recall the advice of R. C. Trench in the appendix of this study: an accurate interpretation of a parable leaves none of the main circumstances or details unexplained. To illustrate, Trench points out, "a harp is not all strings and a knife is not all edge." We could extend this illustration for "fruit" by noting that an apple is not all red, and there is more to a banana than its peel.

In the same sense "fruit", in this parable, is more than simply the evidence of the Spirit (the gifts of the Holy Spirit) in one's life, in fact, it is much more.

The primary focus in this parable is reproduction -- the act of producing a harvest by sowing seed, or the act of producing other Christians by spreading the Word.

It must be noted, however, that the *fruit of the Spirit* and *reproductive fruit* are inseparable qualities of *whole fruit*, one cannot exist without the other -- they are integral parts of a whole (like a banana and peel or an apple and core).

Reproductive fruit cannot be born without the germination of the fruits of the Spirit and you cannot have the fruits of the Spirit without eventually germinating and reproducing -- in other words, bringing others to Christ. So the fruits of the Spirit and leading others to Christ go hand in hand, one cannot exist long without evidence of the other appearing also.

Jesus' specific focus, in this parable, is on the reproductive aspect of fruit. But even more than that it is the fact that *fruit* is essential to being a Christian -- there is no such thing as a sterile or barren Christian.

Highlighting his own reproductive capacity, Paul said, "Onesimus have I *begotten* in the faith." This verb in the Greek clearly signifies *birth*. Sheep beget sheep, nowhere does the Bible claim that the shepherd begets the sheep. Likewise, Christians beget Christians.

This word, "begotten," in these verses is also the Greek one rendered "begotten" in John 3:16. The difference is that one is a physical birth and the other a spiritual birth. It clearly admits to our co-labors with the Holy Spirit in persuading people to new birth in Christ. Again, there is no such thing as a sterile or barren Christian.

6. Is their fruit in your life? If so, explain. If not, what does the lack of fruit tell you about your "Christian" faith and what are you going to do about it?

Have you influenced others to a point where they have also entered into a reconciled relationship with Christ? If not, do not be deceived, the only remedy is in adjusting the aim of your supreme intention of heart -- *your purpose for living*. What is it, Jesus' goals or something else?

Some may protest this dreadful implication by pointing to services they have performed with their time, talent, and finances; dedicated to missions, singing in the choir, driving church buses, teaching Sunday school, visiting the sick and other subordinate ministries of the Church. These services, and more, are all important ministries that should not be set aside unless they have become a substitute and excuse for the neglect of our primary purpose -- persuading others to repentance and new life in Christ. The neglect of this foremost responsibility renders any secondary ministries of no eternal value. Such service may even become damnable in the eyes of God if allowed to continue without being put in proper perspective to the primary goals of Christ.

God is vitally more interested in what you can do to bring souls into His Kingdom than whether you play an instrument, teach Sunday School, lead music, or perform other church services. There is questionable hope for those who routinely attend church functions yet cannot point to others they have influenced for Christ.

This is the kind of self-deception found among those whose hearts are "thorny ground"-- the Kadesh-Barnea type so prevalent in churches.

Concerning deceivers and self-deceived, Jesus remarks: "You will know them by their fruits. Are grapes gathered from thorns, or figs from thistles? In the same way, every good tree bears good fruit. A good tree cannot bear bad fruit, nor can a bad tree bear good fruit. Every tree that does not bear good fruit is cut down and thrown into the fire. Thus you will know them by their fruits.

Not everyone who says to me, "Lord, Lord," will enter the kingdom of heaven, but only the one who does the will of my Father in heaven. On that day many will say to me, "Lord, Lord, did we not prophesy in your name, and do many deeds of power in your name?" Then I will declare to them, "I never knew you; go away from me, you evildoers." (Matthew 7:16-23).

7. List the traits of those who will enter the Kingdom of Heaven, and the traits and words of those to whom Jesus will say, "I never knew you, go away from me, you evildoers."

8. Jesus said, "you will know them by their fruits" If someone were to describe you by your fruits, would they say your fruit was good, or bad or would they question whether you had any fruit ? Why?

8

Examining Ourselves And Our Message, The Seed

In this chapter we will consider different manners of spreading the gospel, some which are valid and some which are not, which ones produce genuine new believers in Christ and which ones are symbolized in the parable by a sower sowing in poor soil.

It is one thing to recognize that there is no vital Christianity without reproducing new life in Christ in another. But it is quite another thing to know how valid 'new life' (or valid reproduction) is to be made.

> "If our Gospel message is itself corrupted by the very ideas it is called upon to combat, then indeed we are in a dangerous condition. The urgent necessity to proclaim the Christian message in an unchristian world is obvious. But, in a logical sense, it is subordinate and secondary to the need to keep the Christian message Christian, and if it isn't now truly a Christian message, we must avail ourselves of the completed Biblical research for its restoration now."[1]

1. Look up Mark 4:8-9, 20. What are the different percentages of fruit harvested from good soil by the different sowers?

2. What reason(s) can you think of that might explain the differences in the percentage of fruit harvested on *good soil*?

1. By Harry Conn. From a paper prepared for the 1992 Evangelistic Education Ministries conference, titled *Gordon Olson's Methods of Research of the Foreknowledge of God.*

There are many conceivable reasons for the different percentages of fruit harvested from good soil. However, the Bible does not spell out the exact reasons, only that there is a difference and that it has nothing to do with the soil because *the soil is good.* In other words, the conditions of heart in the hearers is receptive and willing, so the fault for a low harvest cannot be blamed on them.

3. In your mind, re-examine the types of harvest,(if any),that arise from sowing on the path, stony ground and among thorns. Can you think of any methods of sowing that could have been partially or altogether responsible?

As you read through the 3 categories found in the opposite column below, consider yourself as the sower, and examine yourself carefully. Ask the Holy Spirit to run His search light through you to see if there are any faulty ways in you or your manner of spreading the gospel (sowing).

Pay special attention to yourself in this examination. You are responsible for you and only you can change you and what you do. You are not responsible for anyone else and you cannot change and control anyone else; nor, are they responsible for you nor can they change and control you. Focus on whom you can control and change--*you*!

<u>The Path</u>

What farmer would purposely sow his crops on a path? Once seed is sown on a path, can it be watered, plowed, irrigated, or fertilized, can it be tended in any worthwhile fashion while it remains on a path? Is there much sense to this farming procedure? Conceivably, one could accidentally scatter some seed on a path but what kind of farmer would carelessly scatter seed without trying to get most in the field and as little as possible on the path?

What thoughtful Christian would present the glorious Gospel of our Lord Jesus Christ this way?

There is no sense in that kind of sowing. Yet this is precisely the way inaccurate, illogical, superficial interpretations of the Gospel develop and spread.

Those who are not thorough; not really aware of the seriousness of what they are doing, deliver the Gospel message in this manner. They may have zeal, but they have not realized the gravity of preaching and teaching Good News.

Then there is the procrastinating farmer, the one who does not really like his vocation. He waits until the last minute to put in the seed, until it is almost too late in the season. He is so rushed and bothered that he does a sloppy job. He gets his seed in the field, all over the path, rocks, thorns and everywhere else at the same time. He does not really care, he just wants to get it done.

Likewise some "Christians" avoid the whole thought of spreading the gospel. They put it off and find excuses for as long as possible until they are overcome by the weight of conviction. By then, they feel so delinquent that they take no time to prepare. Bursting at the seams they toss the seed without even noticing where it lands. Their urgent interest is in relieving their personal guilt that has built up through neglecting their responsibility. They do not take care whether the seed takes root, they simply do not want to *look* irresponsible, they do not want to *look* like a "Christian who does not care about others."

Sowing on the path always proves futile. Satan steals the seed because the soil is so calloused and hard the seed cannot find a soft place of refuge beneath its surface, but also because the sower was too rushed, lazy, or indifferent to present the gospel seed in a manner that it could take hold.

Being consumed with ourselves, how easy it is to "sow on the path." In the case of the seed sown along the path, not only are the hearers apathetic and irresponsible, but the sowers are too. They do not know enough about the Truth and seriousness of the Gospel to present it correctly and they do not care.

The ones sown along the path never believe because they receive a lackadaisical presentation of the Gospel and do not understand it and they do not care enough to go after Truth on their own.

Do *you* really love God with *all your heart*? If so, you will naturally desire to lead others to new birth in Him--it is a joy and a delight because this is what we are designed to do when we are cleansed and restored to salvation ourselves. We are designed to reproduce.

Not all sowing procedures are as blatantly wrong as those of the sower who just does not care. There are other manners of spreading the gospel that stem from great intentions, sincere effort and expectations but the results are lousy. These are not so obvious.

Cheap Grace

Most of us at one time or another have been distressed over the condition of some unbeliever's heart. In the process we become anxious for their welfare because their very life is at stake and we feel something immediate must be done about it.

In this frame of mind, one is consumed with the welfare of the unbeliever, and becomes anxious and rushed because lives are at stake. There is hardly time to pray.

As a natural response to the fear that drives the message, everyone who hears it is expected to make a binding commitment to Christ after only a brief presentation of the Gospel. In fact, the briefer and more urgent the message the better because the important thing is to shuffle dying individuals away from the gates of hell and into the gates of heaven as quickly as possible. A common procedure is to rush through a tract, tell an emotional story and invite a person to "ask Jesus into his heart." If the person agrees, he is asked to repeat a prayer, encouraged to read the Bible and go to church -- case closed.

The sower feels an overwhelming sense of relief believing another person has been ushered into God's hands while the hearer may be left a bit bewildered.

The problem is simple. Asking anyone to pray life-long-vows in dedication to Jesus after only a 10 or 20 minute introduction is like arranging a wedding between an adult and a 4 year old and later wondering why the marriage is not working.

Nevertheless the prevailing argument defending rushed invitations is that "the hearer may die tonight."

4. **Look up 2 Peter 3:9. What is God's will? What is not God's will?**

Fearing the impending death of an unenlightened unbeliever is not altogether scriptural. The argument overlooks God's declaration that He is not willing that any should perish but that all should come to repentance and to the knowledge of Him.

When an unbeliever begins to show evidence of genuine interest in God, showing a desire to turn to Him in repentance for salvation, no matter how small, it is reasonable to rely on God's will to preserve his life in safety until he has enough understanding of the gospel to make an intelligent decision one way or another.

God's mercy, on the other hand, *may not be presumed upon* to linger as long *for the one who clearly understands the Gospel but intentionally stalls from surrender to Christ* in order to drink up the last dregs of selfishness before converting (II Peter 2:9, 10). This one's interest in Jesus is not genuine but calculated and selfish. He wants the world and heaven too but does not care much about Christ.

5. **Look up Hebrews 11:1. What is faith the substance of? What is faith the conviction of?**

6. **Look up I John 4:18. What casts out all fear? What does fear have to do with (what is it's substance)?**

Think hard! concerning both of the preceding verses in the last two questions then consider the following statement:

God's love for us is perfect love. His Perfect Love was displayed on the Cross and as He rose from the dead. This Perfect Act of Love has abolished any reason for a fear of punishment by those who are reconciled to Him because the ultimate punishment is death and Christ's perfect love has conquered death. He acted as our substitute, He took our punishment, by giving His Life on The Cross and rising again to life.

When we come to realize and receive God's Perfect Love all fear is cast away (even the fear of death). This is a fact for anyone and everyone who will turn to His Perfect Love in faith. Faith in His Perfect Love and fear of death cannot exist together in the same heart at the same time.

7. Read over the two different styles for presenting the gospel as they appear in the opposite column on the next page and decide which one you think would be most effective. Which one is more in keeping with God's character, His promises and the Bible. Circle your answer A or B.

(A.) Or **(B.)**

(A.) Sharing the Gospel in faith (not fear) and presenting it completely and clearly (no matter how long it takes):

Faith in His desire that is not willing that anyone should perish.

Faith in His longing that everyone should turn in repentance and find new life in Him.

Faith in His perfect love, that will not condemn anyone to eternal death who has not *purposefully* rejected Him to hold on to their own sin and selfishness.

(B.) Sharing the Gospel quickly, and briefly (emphasizing mainly the benefits) out of the fear "the hearer may die tonight:"

Fear that indicates one should turn to God just to avoid hell.

Fear that implies God is impatient, arbitrary, unreasonable, unbending, cruel and unloving.

Fear that presumes a thoughtlessly repeated prayer gives a person a rite of passage into heaven with a license to continue in known sin on earth.

Being relaxed and unhurried in *faith* gives credibility to our message and to the loving-kindness of our Great God (Heb. 4:1-2).

Again, who would rush anyone he just met to the altar and marry that person for fear she might die tonight? When you truly love someone you want that person to be sure she really loves you too before you marry.

As we spread the Word, how much more should we want to be sure that those we "take to the altar and wed to Jesus" are sure they love Him?

A Gospel of Cheap Grace Is Disgrace to God

The Israelites said to Isaiah, "prophesy unto us smooth things" (Isaiah 30:10). They wanted to skip the convicting truth that demanded a change in their lives and jump straight to the benefits they could receive from God.

Most people are the same today, wanting to know how they can benefit from the gospel while being spared the stinging conviction that requires a change of heart. But, unlike Isaiah, many sowers give people exactly what they want.

Everyone wants to be liked, but a dominant fear for not hurting peoples feelings and making them dislike you abruptly renders our message polite but powerless. Unswerving devotion and love for God and our fellow man requires us to place the unbelievers' feelings at the foot of the Cross, and honestly (but gently) uncover all hiding places for sin.

Understandably, yet sadly, many Christians shrink from this thorough task and settle for spreading something diluted and more appealing--some benefit of Christianity--an incentive which will insure the unbeliever's interest and maintain thc "likableness" of the sower.

The problem is that the benefits alone are NOT CHRISTIANITY. One cannot receive the benefits without counting the cost or meeting the conditions! We must take every precaution to be sure that those who listen to our good news understand the real Gospel, not just its benefits.

Venturing to proclaim the benefits of Truth without clearly explaining the Truth and the way to it, is a sure formula for tragedy in the hearer.

The responsibility of "sowing" must never be taken lightly or with a view to maintaining our personal popularity or preserving the feelings of an unbeliever concerning sin.

We must never take for granted that those with whom we share automatically understand the condition most frequently ignored in spreading the gospel--a change of heart.[1] Change of heart is essential, it is absolutely necessary in the one who wants to take Jesus as Savior. You cannot have salvation without it. This change of heart is most commonly referred to as repentance in the Bible.

No one can understand and receive the Good News until he or she has understood the bad news first. The bad news is that without God we are selfish, degenerate little people. The Good News is we can be changed, we can have a new life in Christ with a new reason for living. No longer do we need to live for ourselves and our petty selfishness, we can turn from that life and turn to Christ, and through faith receive new life in Him, with peace and joy everlasting.

A sower may have access to vast fields of good soil, (receptive hearts), but if the sower attempts to leave out repentance and the need to forsake sin, the field will soon fill with weeds, stones and thorns, and will choke the present fruit and fail to produce more.

8. Find and read again Mr. Conn's quote at the beginning of this chapter then explain what it means in reference to what we have learned about sowing on various soils.

9. Why do you think so many *rocks* and *horns* exist in the Church today?

10. Is there such a thing as optional or partial discipleship? Why or why not? (Support your answer with scripture).

1. *A change of heart* is more than a change of mind. A change of mind is simply changing from one way of thinking to another. It is easy to change one's mind to agree that Jesus is Christ and the Christian life is preferable to any other but a *change of heart* requires also a change in lifestyle, *actually living the Christian life,* simply agreeing with it is inadequate. The Bible calls *a change of heart repentance.*

11. How do you intend to spread the gospel yet avoid bringing rocky and stony hearts into the Church?

The disciples, initially, may have thought that the four conditions of heart, represented by the four kinds of soil, were permanently fixed. But no heart is impenetrable by design, only by the choice of the owner. Even for those who have brought themselves into an evil, stony, or thorny condition of heart, recovery is still possible through repentance and the grace of God-- the hard soil may become soft; the shallow deep; the soil beset with thorns made clear.

12. From now on, whenever you have an opportunity to influence another concerning the gospel what key points do you want to emphasize? What "styles" or "techniques" do you want to avoid?

Part 2

Interpreting Other Parables By The Key Parable

1
Two Proverbial Paradigms

We have concluded part one of our study on Jesus' first parable, *The Parable of the Sower.* In that portion of our study we learned that *The Parable of the Sower* is the key to understanding all of His parables which is why Jesus shared it first. Jesus ends *The Parable of the Sower* by describing the results of sowing on good soil, in other words, sharing the gospel with those whose hearts are open and receptive to it.

In Mark's gospel, Jesus sums up the traits of the seed sown in good soil with a metaphor found in Mark 4:21.

Look up Mark 4:21.

Think about what the light or lamp symbolizes in Mark 4:21 and consider the context of the following scriptures that refer to "light."

<u>JESUS CHRIST PUT THE LIGHT OF GOD ON EXHIBITION:</u>

- I have come down from heaven, not to do My own will, but the will of Him who sent Me (John 6:38).
- He who has seen Me has seen the Father (John 1:18; 14:9-11).
- I am the light of the world (John 8:12).
- The life was the light of men (John 1:4). -- perfection of motive and conduct demonstrated.
- He who follows Me shall not walk in the darkness, but shall have the light of life (John 8:12).

THOSE RECONCILED TO GOD ARE NOW THE LIGHT OF THE WORLD (Matthew 5:14). (They became such by allowing the light of God's truth to expose their past life of darkness and then turning to God in repentance and faith.)

- I am come that they might have life, said the Savior (John 10:10).
- Now you are light in the Lord; walk as children of light (Eph. 5:8).
- You are all sons of light and sons of day (1 Thess. 5:5).
- If we walk in the light as He Himself is in the light, we have fellowship with one another (1John 1:7).
- He who practices the truth comes to the light (John 3:21).
- Let your light shine before men in such a way that they may see your good works, and glorify your Father who is in heaven (Matthew 5:16).
- And this is the message we have heard from Him and declare to you: God is light; in Him there is no darkness at all. If we claim to have fellowship with Him yet walk in darkness, we lie and do not live by the truth. But if we walk in the light as He is in the light, we have fellowship with one another, and the blood of Jesus, His Son, purifies us from all sin (1 John 1:5-7).

God is light! He is therefore the source of all virtuous enlightenment. All things become visible when they are exposed by the light (Ephesians 5:13).

1. Refer to Mark 4:21 again. What do you think Jesus meant by *light* or *lamp* in this proverbial paradigm?

The lamp (light) in this proverb represents understanding, comprehension of the Gospel indicated by new Life in a Christian. It is enlightenment.

The next object with a figurative meaning in Mark 4:21 is the bushel (or bowl). This one may be more difficult to interpret because its symbolism is not recognized as well today as when it was written. But here is a hint: In the United States, on the Thanksgiving Holiday, a cornucopia, also called a "horn of plenty," is often filled to overflowing with fruit and vegetables as a symbol representing the occasion and what it commemorates. The cornucopia, as a symbol, is very similar in its meaning to that of the bushel in our metaphor.

2. What do you think the bushel (or bowl) represents? What does it mean?

3. The next figurative subject is the bed. What does it represent?

One would not light a lamp and place it under a bushel, in other words, hide it by a life concentrated in materialism and gain. This could also apply to a full or busy life--not enough time for the Gospel. The bed represents relaxation and ease and corresponds to a life of leisure or luxury. This is directed toward those who understand the Gospel, yet whose faith and dedication are buried under a life of convenience, materials, or laziness.

God gladly illumines our minds to His truth, but He will not give understanding to the rebellious, distracted, or lazy. God will not further enlighten anyone who is going to hold the light within for himself only, anymore than a person in his right mind would light a candle and put it under a bed or bushel!

When we receive enlightenment, we must conform to that truth in obedience and respond to its burning demand to be passed on to others. If the lamp which Christ came to light has in any sense lighted our life, we cannot rest until we light as many other lives as possible.

4. Look up Matthew 5:16 and write it in the space below.

It is one thing to know there is no vital Christianity without The Light (Christ) which has come into the world; it is another to know how that light in us (Christian lifestyle) is to be shined. Our testimony shines not by telling *who* we are but *whose* we are.

5. Whom (or what) does our testimony (light) say we belong to when it is hidden under a bushel or a bed?

In *The Parable of The Sower* we learned of the pitfalls of sowing on soil that was hard, rocky or thorny, but what about hostile, eruptive ground? Let's look at another bit of wisdom in Matthew 7:6.

6. Look up Matthew 7:6. What do you think Jesus meant by this warning?

7. Look up Proverbs 23:9. How is this similar to Jesus' proverb in Matthew 7:6?

Christ warns us in Matthew 7:6 not to reveal too much truth to those who are unworthy or hostile, lest they turn and tear us apart verbally or physically. This rule simply means to avoid revealing more truth than people are ready to receive.

When we carelessly toss out pearls (truth) it can backfire. Rather than influencing and persuading some people toward Christ, premature words of wisdom can further harden them from receiving truth, plus they may react by trying to harm us.

The best way to approach hardened, hostile people is to first pray for them and continue to pray and watch until you see the soil of their hearts begin to soften and become more open to the gospel. Follow the Holy Spirit's leading as you pray and watch for the right opportunity to reveal your pearls of truth.

2
Tares, Nets, & Vines

In Part 1 of this workbook we reviewed the fact that an extra key is necessary to unlocking the Parables of Jesus. That extra key is simply the correct interpretation of the first parable, *The Parable of the Sower.* Jesus himself said, "Do you not understand this parable? Then how will you understand all of the parables (Mark 4:13)?

You should have gained a thorough understanding of the key parable, *The Parable of the Sower*, in Part 1 of this workbook. Now, let's test our understanding of *The Parable of the Sower*, to see if it helps us understand another parable, *The Parable of the Tares.*

Read Matthew 13:24-30.

The similarity of this parable to *The Parable of the Sower* is evident. *The Parable of the Tares* is also an account of someone sowing seed in a field, but here the four types of hearts symbolized by different soils exist intermingled. As the scene unfolds an enemy sows weeds (tares) in the field while those in charge are asleep. When the cruel act is discovered, the caretakers conclude both the weeds and the grain must be left to grow together until harvest, otherwise some good could be uprooted with the bad. Finally, at harvest, they are gathered into separate bundles and the weeds are burned while the grain is stored.

2. Review Matthew 13:36-43 and note what each symbol stands for in the opposite column.

Sower

Field

Good seed

Weeds

Enemy

Harvest

Reapers

The Parable of the Sower and *The Parable of the Tares* are so closely related that when taken together they increase our understanding.[1]

Let's look at the *tares* in this parable since they were not mentioned in *The Parable of the Sower.* Again, scholar, R. C. Trench, enlightens us.

The wheat and tares are not from seeds totally unalike. They are more like a mock hybrid -- the tares being a wild wheat. The poisonous darnel (lolium temulentum) is a weed which, botanically, is closely related to bearded wheat, and in the early stages of growth they are hard to tell apart. They do not appear to be different until they have brought forth their fruit.

1. Emphasizing the strategy for increased understanding, Trench writes, "When our Lord Himself interpreted the two first [parables] ..., the sower and the tares, ... He intended to furnish us with a key to interpret them all. (16) While all teaching , worthy the name, has power to take root in the hearts of hearers, in a higher sense this must be true of the words which He spoke Who was Himself the Seminal Word... the Lord intended to set Himself forth as the Chief Sower of Seed. His was a going forth to sow; the Word was His seed; the hearts of men His soil." (29, 30) - R.C. Trench, *Notes on the Parables of Our Lord*, (Grand Rapids, MI: Baker Book House, 1980), p. 16, 29, 30.

In *The Parable of the Tares,* both the wheat and the tares are allowed to grow together until the time of the harvest. Why? Because until the seeds mature and bear fruit, the plants are difficult to tell apart, and some good sprouts could be uprooted with the bad. The difference between the wheat and weeds is only apparent when the ear is formed; thus fulfilling literally the Lord's words, "by their fruits you shall know them."

2. Besides good sprouts uprooted with the bad what could be another drastic result from trying to separate the good and bad before harvest?

3. Look up I Samuel 16:7. How does this relate to what we are learning in *The Parable of the Tares*? How does mankind judge things?

4. Now read I Corinthians 4:5. How does this compare to Matthew 13:28,29?

5. Recall the two young men desiring to become pastors (Part I, p. 5). How does *The Parable of the Tares* reinforce what we learned about supreme motive of heart and it's "visibility?"

Why is so much patience until the harvest necessary? Because people are not capable of making the separation effectively (Mt. 13:29). Like wild, mock wheat and true wheat are indistinguishable until they bear fruit, so are true and false believers. Mere mankind are not capable of consistently and accurately discerning the heart; if they attempt to make separations, they will inevitably commit errors of judgment and root up good wheat with the tares while retaining some tares with the good.Satan's battle scheme is infiltration by imitation. It would be useless to sow weeds among weeds in his own camp. Satan sows the wicked in the Church by imitating the righteous. There most of these "tares" remain (until Judgment) because the separation cannot be accurately carried out by mere man.

The wheat and tares are indistinguishable outwardly in the same way the outward choices and actions of people are often indistinguishable and do not always reflect their true inner heart motivation. Many are not the Lord's, yet resemble those who are: they go to church, pray, read the Bible like Christians, but are Christless. For this reason, Jesus said to let them grow together until the time when they bear fruit, then they will be harvested according to their product, the fruit. The fruit alone will reveal their inner ultimate intention of heart.

6. In what order is the gathering and bundling at harvest?

The fact that the tares are gathered first has interesting implications. In the "religious community," the bundling together is apparent. Protestants, Catholics and Jews fraternize with New-agers, Hindus and Buddhists and the doctrine of unity is their gospel theme. Could it be the Divine Command to "gather the tares in bundles" has already gone forth?

Though unity between religions seems progressive, it is the exact opposite when pursued in place of the gospel, (or, as the gospel), in those extremes where unity is sought at the expense of foundational beliefs.

7. Quickly read over *The Parable of the Net* in Matthew 13:47-50. What happens after the net is drawn and the fish are pulled to shore?

8. How is this the same as what Jesus said would happen to the tares and wheat at the harvest? Compare *The Parable of the Net* to *The Parable of the Tares* with regard to separation and judgment.

The net referred to in this parable has a name in the original language that distinguishes it from the average fishing net. This net can extend as far as a half mile in length and is weighted so that it sweeps the ocean bottom while the top, being supported by floating corks, skims the surface. It is designed to draw in everything from top to bottom for a great distance.

The far-embracing span of the net represents the potentially wide reach of the gospel. Here the fishers take fish of all kinds within the folds of the net; men of all shades of moral character have the gospel preached to them, and find themselves within the visible Church.

The moral of this parable, *The Parable of the Net*, is different from that of the Tares. It reveals to us that we should not be content simply with being enclosed in the Gospel-net,--because "they are not all Israel who are of Israel,"--"the Lord knows them that are his," and will one day bring all confusion to an end, separating forever the "precious from the vile."

9. Describe the variations in the meanings of these two parables, *The Parable of the Sower* and *The Parable of the Tares.* Remember each parable carries only one essential meaning though it may have thousands of applications.

The symbolism in both of these parables, The Sower and The Tares, are so similar that liberty is expected in comparing the two, though the essential focus of each parable varies.

The Parable of the Sower focuses on the characteristics of Christians in contrast with "Christian sympathizers." The moral of the parable is: there is no such thing as a sterile or barren Christian -- Christians are known by their fruit.

The Parable of the Tares, on the other hand, contrasts the destiny of true Christians with that of "Christian- sympathizers" and others. The moral is that patience in waiting for the time of separating is crucial.

In spite of the variations, both parables point condemningly not only to those with evidence of sin in their lives but also to those who presumptuously bear the name "Christian." Even those who have attended church for 5, 10, even 20 years but are unable to identify any whom they have influenced in some way to become a believer in Christ. Such individuals have every reason to doubt whether they are "eternally secure" members of God's Kingdom!

According to both parables--*The Sower and The Tares*--The fruit is the deciding factor. There is no such thing as a sterile, barren Christian.

Isaiah 5:1-4 serves as another candid reminder of God's unchanging purpose regarding fruitfulness. It describes an agricultural setting with striking resemblance to *The Parables of the Sower and Tares.*

Read Isaiah 5:1-4 and answer the following questions:

10. What kind of soil was the vineyard planted on (Isaiah 5:1-4)? What does this tell you?

11. How did the vineyard owner care for the ground? What does this tell you?

12. What did the ground yield at harvest? What does this tell you?

13. **What was the Vineyard Keeper's response and why?**

14. **What did the Vineyard Owner do to ensure a good harvest?**

15. **What more could the Vineyard Owner have done?**

In this account, the Vineyard Owner made all the proper preparations for His vineyard to yield a bountiful harvest. The location was a very fertile hill corresponding to the good soil of good hearts. Plus everything possible had been done to enhance the fertility of the vineyard and assure the development of its produce.

All this care proved futile. The Vineyard Owner, God, did not get the crop He expected. Wild grapes (tares) grew up instead. The vine, by rejecting the Vineyard Owner's care, could mature to nothing more than a worthless wild weed.

Disappointed, the Vineyard Owner exclaims, "... Judge between Me and My vineyard. What more was there to do for My vineyard that I have not done in it?"

"In order for the seed of God to produce fruit it must be planted in an honest and good heart, a heart of willing faith, and a love of God. This speaks of our ultimate intention or primary purpose in living: either for the happiness and well-being of God and our fellowman, or ourselves. It also speaks of "singleness of eye," or making the truth of God our "focal point." It pertains not only to how we hear and perceive the Word, but also how we live out the truth we hear and perceive (Luke 11:34).

Finally we understand the importance of proper soil preparation, not just in our own lives, as having the seed sown in us, but also as we go forth to sow the seed of the Word. We must be certain that we are preparing someone else's heart-soil so that they may come along side us in understanding and consecration.[1]

---

1. Ken Schultz- founder The Tawala Bible School, Papua New Guinea, Men for Missions, P.O. Box 6109, Minneapolis, MN.

16. Now look up John 15:1-9. Who is the Vine in this analogy? Who is the Vinedresser? Who are the branches?

17. What does the Vinedresser do to branches that do <u>not</u> bear fruit?

18. What does He do to branches that <u>do</u> bear fruit?

19. Review verse 3 of John 15.According to this verse, what can you determine about the pruning process?

20. Compare John 15:6 to the *bundles* in the Parable of the Tares (Matthew 13:30). How are they alike?

21. How is God glorified?

Jesus Christ descended to earth as a man born of a virgin to show us how to live a perfect life in relation to God and each other. Then He gave His life and rose from the dead that by His suffering on our behalf we might have new opportunity through repentance and faith to be restored to a proper relationship with God, and our fellowman. What more could He do for us, His vineyard?

Jesus referred to Himself as the Vine; His Father as the Vinedresser; and to us as the branches (John 15).

We, as branches, individually bear good fruit, wild fruit (tares), or nothing. To ensure that we are branches bearing good fruit, we must meet the conditions for receiving all that He has provided for us by means of repentance and faith. We must also continue in love with Him with all of our heart, mind, soul and strength.

Judge now between Christ, and His vineyard (You!). What more was there He could do for you, that He has not done?

22. **How will you, as a branch in His vineyard, respond to what Jesus Christ has done for you? (Give a thorough answer and remember, *you will be known by your fruit!*).**

3
Feasts and Weddings

In this chapter we look at three parables of similar settings--*The Parable of the Great Feast* (Luke 14:16-24), and *The Parable of the King's Wedding for His Son* (Matthew 22:1-14), and *The Parable of the Ten Virgin Bridesmaids* (Matthew 25:1-13).

1. Read Luke 14:1-24. In verse 1, note the day, and setting. Also note what Jesus was doing and whom He was with.

2. Review verses 7-14 of Luke Chapter 14. What did Jesus notice in verse 7, and what did He tell the guests?

3. Who was Jesus' host and what did Jesus tell him?

4. How would you feel if you were the host or one of the guests? Do you think they were comfortable while Jesus told them these things?

In verse 15 we are told that a guest (who may have been trying to ease the tension by redirecting the conversation) commented to Jesus, "Blessed is the man who will cat at the feast in the kingdom of God." It is this remark that sets the context for *The Parable of the Great Feast.*

5. Since verse 15 set the context for *The Parable of the Feast,* where can we assume Jesus intended His hearers to think the feast in this parable would take place?

6. How many of the original guests in the parable made excuses for not being able to attend?[1]

   What was the first excuse?
   What was the second excuse?
   What was the third?

7. Are any of these excuses "sin?" Explain.

Since we know that ***all*** of the original, invited guests made excuses we can presume that this was only a partial list of excuses made. The point is that ***all of the excuses*** provoked the One giving the feast. None was sufficient to miss this dinner party.

8. Compare the "excuse making" in this parable to the soils in *The Parable of the Sower.* Match the excuses to the soils by placing the number of the excuse in the blank before the type of soil to which it corresponds.

Excuse 1--buying unseen land
Excuse 2--buying oxen
Excuse 3--got married

________the soil of a hardened path
________rocky soil
________thorny soil
________good soil

1. It is poor business for a man to buy property he has not seen. But the second excuse shows even less prudence, for oxen could be old, and incapable of being renewed like land. The third is the worst excuse of all, he could have left his wife for a few hours as he did, no doubt, on many occasions. He was not asked to divorce his wife, simply to attend a banquet.

The Jews believed that the resurrection and the setting up of the heavenly kingdom, would begin with a great festival, of which all the Jewish community would be partakers. The guest who remarked to Jesus, "Blessed and holy is he that has part in the first resurrection," most likely, took it for granted that he should be one of the privileged at that feast. He did not pause to consider whether he had truly accepted the conditions of the invitation. Neither did he consider that his refusal of Christ's call to a higher spiritual life would ensure his personal and final rejection from that heavenly festival. To him, and to others like him, the parable was spoken.[1]

9. What parallel connections do these excuses have with the words of Jesus that follow soon after in Luke 14:26?

Look up I Corinthians 7:29-31.

10. What similarities can you note in Paul's advice compared to the excuses made in *The Parable of the Great Feast*?

11. All of the reasons behind the excuses are common in everyday life and, in themselves, are not wrong. What is it that makes them wrong in the instance of *The Parable of the Great Feast*?

12. In what context would these excuses (or any others) become wrong in your life?

"...And they all with one consent (or, of one mind or spirit) began to make excuse." He who said *"I have bought a piece of ground, and I must go and see it,"* represents those who are elate of heart through acquired possessions.

1. R.C. Trench, *Notes on the Parables of Our Lord*, (Grand Rapids, MI: Baker Book House, 1980), p. 127.

It adds much to the earnestness of the warning of the parable that none of the guests are kept away because of occupations which are in themselves sinful. Yet all become sinful, because first priority is given to them. While with one it is "the lust of the eye and the pride of life," that keep him from Christ, in the second it is rather the care and anxiety of business which fills and chokes the soul; *I have bought five yoke of oxen, and I need to try them out.*

In the last we see that it is the pleasure of the world that keeps him from Christ: "Don't you see that I have a feast of my own? Why bother me with yours? *I have married a wife, and therefore I cannot come."* This one accounts that he has a perfectly good reason, and therefore does not trouble himself with the words, *please, have me excused,* but bluntly refuses.

There is an ascending scale. The first guest would be very glad to come, if it were possible; the second alleges no such necessity of absence, but is simply desiring to be excused. The third has plans of his own, and says outright, *I cannot come.*"[1]

Those who made excuses had nothing which was wrong to have, nor were they doing anything which was wrong to do, but undue love of earthly activities and possessions finally excluded them from the feast.

13. How does Luke 14:21 compare to what Jesus told his host in Luke 14:13?

14. What did Christ tell the host the result would be of inviting these to the banquet (verse 14).

We have here a distinct reflection of verse 13. The great Giver of the heavenly feast calls the spiritually sick and needy, while those who are already rich in their own estimation excuse them-selves and are thereby excluded by Him. The publicans and sinners, the despised and outcast of the nation, enter the kingdom of God before those who thanked God they were not as other men.

1. R.C. Trench, *Notes on the Parables of Our Lord*, (Grand Rapids, MI: Baker Book House, 1980), pp. 128, 129.

15. When the master tells the slave to invite the poor, crippled, blind and lame, what is the slave's response in verse 22? Next, what is the master's response? What does this imply concerning whom we are to invite to join Christ and attend His heavenly banquet?

The parable has both historic and prophetic significance. Prophetically, it declares how God will prepare a feast, at which more shall sit down than an exclusive "elect." He has founded a Church in which there would be room for Gentile as well as Jew. This is not directly stated, but is wrapped up in the parable. The servant, returning from his second mission, had said, *Lord, it is done as thou has commanded, and yet there is room,* whereupon, he receives a new commission.

16. What is the new commission received by the servant referred to in the preceding paragraph?

17. Compare this new instruction to the servant with the passage in I Corinthians 1:26-29. What similarities do you note?

The new commission strongly infers that it be made to *all people everywhere* including *pagans* in all senses of the word as well as the apathetic and self-righteous original invitees.

Concerning the third invitation the instruction is, *compel them to come in.* Of course this means a moral compulsion and not a dragging in by force. The idea of compelling does not imply that the newly invited guests would be indifferent to or resist the invitation, but that they might think themselves so unworthy as not to take the invitation seriously. In such a frame of mind they could hardly be convinced without much persuasion that they were invited to the rich man's dwelling, to partake in his feast.

And, since faith cannot be forced, the instruction to compel them must mean the strong, prevailing power of persuasion with which Christians will address others when they are themselves deeply convinced of the importance of their message and of the great results depending upon its spread.

18. Whom do you think the servant sent to bid the guests represents figuratively?

It is interesting to note that the servant sent to bid the guests does not represent Jesus as we might think; neither does he represent the prophets, because he is not sent till "all things are now ready."

The servant(s) sent to bid the guests are those who accompanied Jesus, both then and now. They are preachers, evangelists, apostles, and all who call themselves Christian, after His Name.

19. What is the penalty (consequences) for those who rejected or neglected the invitation (Luke 14:24)?

20. Look up Proverbs 1:28-33, note and compare similarities in this passage to any similarities in the parable.

Now we turn to another parable, *The Wedding Feast given by the King for His Son* found in Matthew 22:1-14. As we read this parable we must keep in mind that in the New Testament culture the distinctions between the engagement (betrothal) and the actual wedding were not as broad as ours are in the West.

The engagement represented every bit as much commitment as the wedding. So, the couple's engagement was viewed as complete commitment to one another while only the celebration remained to take place.

In the West we often distinguish between the engagement and the marriage in an opposite fashion--the engagement period is sometimes perceived as one's last chance to "sow wild oats" before making a "real commitment" at the wedding celebration. Thus many unbecoming bachelor and bachelorette activities often take place in traditional celebration prior to the western wedding ceremony. This is not the case, however, in the *Parable of the King's Wedding for His Son.* The bride and groom are already committed one to another and the guests have "RSVPed," they have accepted the invitation to attending the King's wedding celebration for His Son.

Another Eastern tradition with which Westerners are not familiar was the custom that special garments be worn by the guests in attendance. Guests who accepted an invitation were often expected to wear a special robe or mantle at the celebration. This is somewhat like the western tradition that the bridesmaids and groomsmen wear special attire that sets them apart at the wedding. But at wedding celebrations like the one in our parable *everyone* was expected to wear the required wedding apparel.

21. Read *The Parable of the King's Wedding for His Son* in Matthew 22:1-14. When the King first sent His servants to call those who were invited to the wedding, what was the response?

22. Again, the King sent his servants to call the guests. What were the servants to tell the invited guests this second time?

23. What was the response of those invited twice?

When Christ says to call them that were invited and repeats the invitation declaring, *"All things are now ready,"* He is emphasizing the fact that there was nothing sudden about the coming of His Kingdom. All had ample time to prepare for the festal occasion.

24. What was the King's reaction after the second invitation was rejected?

25. Who did the servants finally bring to the Wedding celebration with the third invitation (Matthew 22:10)?

26. Compare this (Matthew 22:10) to the fish drawn in *The Parable of the Net* and the bundles gathered at harvest in *The Parable of the Tares*? What are the similarities?

27. What did the King notice when He came in to see the guests and how did He respond?

As typical in all parables, the topics hold figurative spiritual meanings that transcend their literal nature. And, in this parable, the idea symbolized by the guest without a wedding garment has spiritual significance. To understand this significance we can refer to the *Actual Great Wedding Feast* represented by this parable as it is described by John in the Book of Revelation when he was given the vision of what was to come.

28. Look up Revelation 19:6-9. Here we are told what the wedding garment(s) stands for. Note the verse in Revelation that reveals what the wedding garment represents and copy it in the space provided.

Let's look at one more wedding parable found in Matthew 25: 1-13, *The Parable of the Ten Virgin Bridesmaids.*

29. Like the other festal parables, what are we told this parable represents (is likened to) according to Matthew 25:1?

30. How many bridesmaids were there? How many were virgins? How many were wise? How many were foolish?

31. What do you think the virginity of the bridesmaids represents?

32. What do you think the bridesmaids' lamps represent? (It may help to review the symbolic significance of *lamp* and *light* covered earlier).

In the East, it is still customary that wedding ceremonies take place at night, so lamps would have been a necessity in Jesus' day. It was also tradition for the groom to retrieve the bride from her home and take her to the place where the ceremony was to be held. The bride and groom would leave her father's house, and the attendants would either accompany them or meet them later at some convenient place on the way.

Although some modern Bible translations leave out the aspect of virginity and refer to the attendants simply as ten bridesmaids, the virgin nature of the bridesmaids should not be overlooked. Their virginity is symbolic of the profession of a pure faith, void of any hint of apostasy from God. In their virginity they represent all professing Christians who are hoping for the return of the Messiah and who do *not* contradict that hope by their lifestyle.

We may consider the foolish virgins as those going through the motions of Christianity, performing external duties, without life, or those who confess Christ with their lips but are not diligent in deeds of humility and love. Merely outward Christian profession is represented by the lamp but the *inward profession* is represented by the oil stored within the lamps--that is the source of true light.

The foolish virgins are not hypocrites or openly ungodly sinners. Rather, the foolish represent the negligent in prayer, the slothful in life. It is not that they have no oil; they have some, just not enough. "In Matthew 13:5, [*The Parable of The Sower*], the seed springs up till the sun scorches it; so here, the lamps burn on till their oil is exhausted."[1] There is evidence of Christian life outwardly but it is not fueled by the rich reserves of deep internal fountains of oil.

The wise virgins, on the other hand, are those who realize that the Church may be awhile before She enters into glory. They realize that they may have an extended period of self-denial, before they shall be called into the heavenly kingdom. They know they must live by principle above feelings if they are to carry on and overcome to the end.[2]

33. While the five foolish virgins are off trying to obtain more sufficient quantity of oil, what happens?

While the foolish were seeking to make up for past neglect, the Bridegroom came, and the wise that were ready, whose lamps were burning, went in with Him to the marriage, and the door was shut. *Afterwards came the other virgins, saying Lord, Lord, open to us.*

1. R.C. Trench, *Notes on the Parables of Our Lord*, (Grand Rapids, Michigan: Baker Book House, 1980), p. 86.
2. R.C. Trench - The information that the bridegroom actually tarried, may be counted as evidence that He would not come for many centuries, then the first ages of the Church would have been deprived of that powerful motive to holiness supplied to each generation... by the possibility of the Lord's return in their time. Prophecy is not fatalism, and **it was [and is] always open to every age by faith and prayer to *hasten* that coming." (2 Pet.3:12),** p. 87.

Having sought for the oil too late, they came looking for mercy. But now had come the time of judgment, the long extended period of mercy and grace (from the death and resurrection of Christ until His return) had passed. The time allotted for mercy culminates with the advent of His return and judgment. Crying, "Lord, Lord," the foolish intend to assert their personal, intimate relation with the Bridegroom hoping thereby to gain access to the kingdom. But *He answers, Truly, I say to you, I know you not.*

Jesus is not denying outward knowledge of the five foolish virgins. He is simply declaring that He never knew them in their innermost being, their heart; nor did they know Him in their hearts. They only knew Him outwardly.

The foolish virgins remain forever excluded from the marriage feast. On this, we may observe that there are four categories of persons:

1.) those that have an *abundant* entrance into heaven,
2.) those that are saved, as though they had been shipwrecked with difficulty reaching shore,
3.) those whose sins go before them on the broad way to destruction,
4.) those who, though they seemed not far from the kingdom, miss it after all.

This was the fate of these five foolish virgins, and it is the most pathetic of all.

Lest that be our fate, the Lord says to us,"*Watch therefore, for ye know neither the day nor the hour;*"... "and this being so, the only certain way of being ready upon *that* day, is that you be ready upon *every* day. Unreadiness upon that day is without remedy. That which would have been the whole of a life cannot be huddled into a moment. *Watch therefore, for ye know neither the day nor the hour.*[1]"

---

1. On this parable in relation to the King's Son's Marriage, and the unworthy guest who finds admission to the marriage feast, while the foolish virgins do not, the marriage festivities spoken of there are different from these. "Those are celebrated in this life in the Church, these at the last day in the Church triumphant. To those, men are called by the Gospel; to these, by the trumpet of the Archangel. To those, who enter, can again go out from them, or be cast out; who is once introduced to these never goes out nor is cast out--thus it is said, *The door was shut.*" - R.C. Trench, *Notes on the Par-ables of Our Lord*, (Grand Rapids, MI: Baker Book House, 1980), p. 90.

We return now to *The Parable of the King's Wedding for His Son* in Matthew 22:1-14.

34. Review Matthew 22:1-14. Were the first servants sent to give the initial invitation the same as those sent with the second invitation? What happened to those who gave the second invitation?

35. Who was sent to avenge the treatment of the 2nd group of servants?

36. Who did the King send forth with the third invitation?

In this parable, as in all the parables, there is a wealth of wisdom concerning many facets of Christendom, from history to prophecy, sin to salvation, heaven to hell, the first coming of Christ to His second, and so forth. The purpose of our study, though, has not been to bring out every gem but simply to determine the primary focus intended by Jesus. Concerning *The Parable of the King's Son's Wedding*, however, it seems appropriate to briefly look at some of the historic and prophetic significance embedded in this parable.

Taking a closer look at the servants in this parable and the way they were treated by those whom they were sent to invite to the wedding, we once again rely heavily on the scholarly works of R.C. Trench as excerpted and edited from his *Notes on the Parables of our Lord.* --

> By the first band of servants is meant John and the Apostles in their first mission--that which they accomplished during the lifetime of our Lord. Initially, the invitation was given without emphasis upon past sin but rather upon the present grace and mercy available (Acts 3:17). And there was no actual maltreatment of these first messengers,--nor was there at the

first against the Lord, nor against the Apostles during His lifetime." Those invited simply would not come.

Concerning the second invitation, there need be no perplexity concerning the words "*other* servants;" for there were many others besides the apostles, such as Stephen, Paul, Barnabas. These went forth as new men, full of the Holy Ghost, not preaching a general kingdom of God, but Christ crucified and His resurrection. Thus they weredeclaring that all things were ready--all the obstacles heaped up by man's sin were removed by God's grace for those who would repent and accept the invitation. In the very blood which had been impiously shed, there was forgiveness of all sins.

Notice also that the king, upon issuing his second invitation, instead of giving threats or rebuke, told his servants only to press the message with greater urgency. *Tell them which are invited,* so that they cannot mistake, *all things are ready. (My oxen and my fatlings are killed).*

But the guests *made light of it, and went their ways, one to his farm, another to his merchandise.* Nor is this the worst; *The remnant took his servants, and treated them spitefully, and slew them.*

As in this parable there are ever in the world two kinds of despisers of the Gospel of God; some who may say, "I pray thee have me excused,"--others in whom it excites feelings of vicious enmity. Those in the first class are again subdivided; for they "went their ways, one to his farm, another to his merchandise." The question naturally arises, Did the Lord intend a distinction? The dangers of *having* ("one to his farm or estate"), and of *getting* ("another to his merchandise"), though cognate, are yet not all the same. There arc those who are full, and there are those who are hoping to be full, of this world; in neither has the divine hunger ever been awakened in the soul.

The remnant took his servants, and treated them spitefully and slew them. The oppositions to the Gospel are not merely worldly, they are also devilish. People despise the Gospel because it wounds their pride, confronts their self-righteousness; reveals their sin and tells them they are accountable to God whether they like it or not. These are other evils in the heart besides worldliness that lead men to vent the hate they have toward God on the bearers of the message.

But when the King heard thereof, he was wroth. The insult was intended for him; and as such, it was avenged; for he *sent forth his armies,...Then saith he to his servants, The wedding is ready, but they which were bidden were not worthy* (compare Acts 13:46). Hereupon the servants *went out into the highways, and gathered all, as many as they found, both bad and good.* In the spirit of this command, Philip went down to Samaria, and Peter baptized Cornelius and his company. When it is said they gathered in "bad" as well as "good," we are not to see in it the explanation of the fact that one should hereafter be found at the festival without a wedding garment. On the contrary, many were *bad* when invited, who through acceptance of the invitation, passed into the number of the *good.*

Few will deny that there are different degrees of moral life, even before obedience to the call of the Gospel. Cornelius or those mentioned in Romans 2:14, are instances of being good, while by bad we mean those who, to man, seem hopelessly gone in moral depravity (see 1 Corinthians 6:9-11). The invitation is accepted by some of both classes; *the wedding was furnished with guests.*

There is still another solemn act of judgment to follow, a second separation. We have had the judgment of the avowed foe; judgment of the false friend is yet to take place. But it is not the servants' office here to make that judgment. *When the King came in to see the guests, he saw there a man which had not on a wedding garment.* Him he addresses, though mildly; for it was yet to be seen whether he could explain his conduct. *Friend, how camest thou in hither, not having a wedding garment?* But he was *speechless.*

The rejection of a gift, or the appearance of a slight put upon it, is typically viewed as a contempt of the giver. But this guest was guilty of a further affront in appearing at the festival in disrespectful apparel. He did not feel that he had anything to say for himself; *he was speechless*, literally, his mouth was stopped; he

> stood self-condemned. *Then said the King to the servants; "bind him hand and foot, and take him away, and cast him into outer darkness..."*
>
> The meaning of the wedding garment and what its lack signifies in this parable has been disputed often. It was righteousness, both in its root of faith and flower of charity. According to Paul's image, here peculiarly appropriate, he had not "put on Christ"-- in which... both faith and charity are included -- the whole adornment of the new and spiritual man. Let us contemplate this guest as a self-righteous man, making and trusting in his own righteousness... a despiser, counting himself good enough in himself, in the flesh, and not in the spirit, to appear before God."[1]

In Trench's above analysis he notes two classes of Gospel-Despisers. These two classes can be further divided into sub-categories as shown in the chart on the following page.

1. R.C. Trench, *Notes on the Parables of Our Lord*, (Grand Rapids, Michigan: Baker Book House, 1980), p. 77-83.

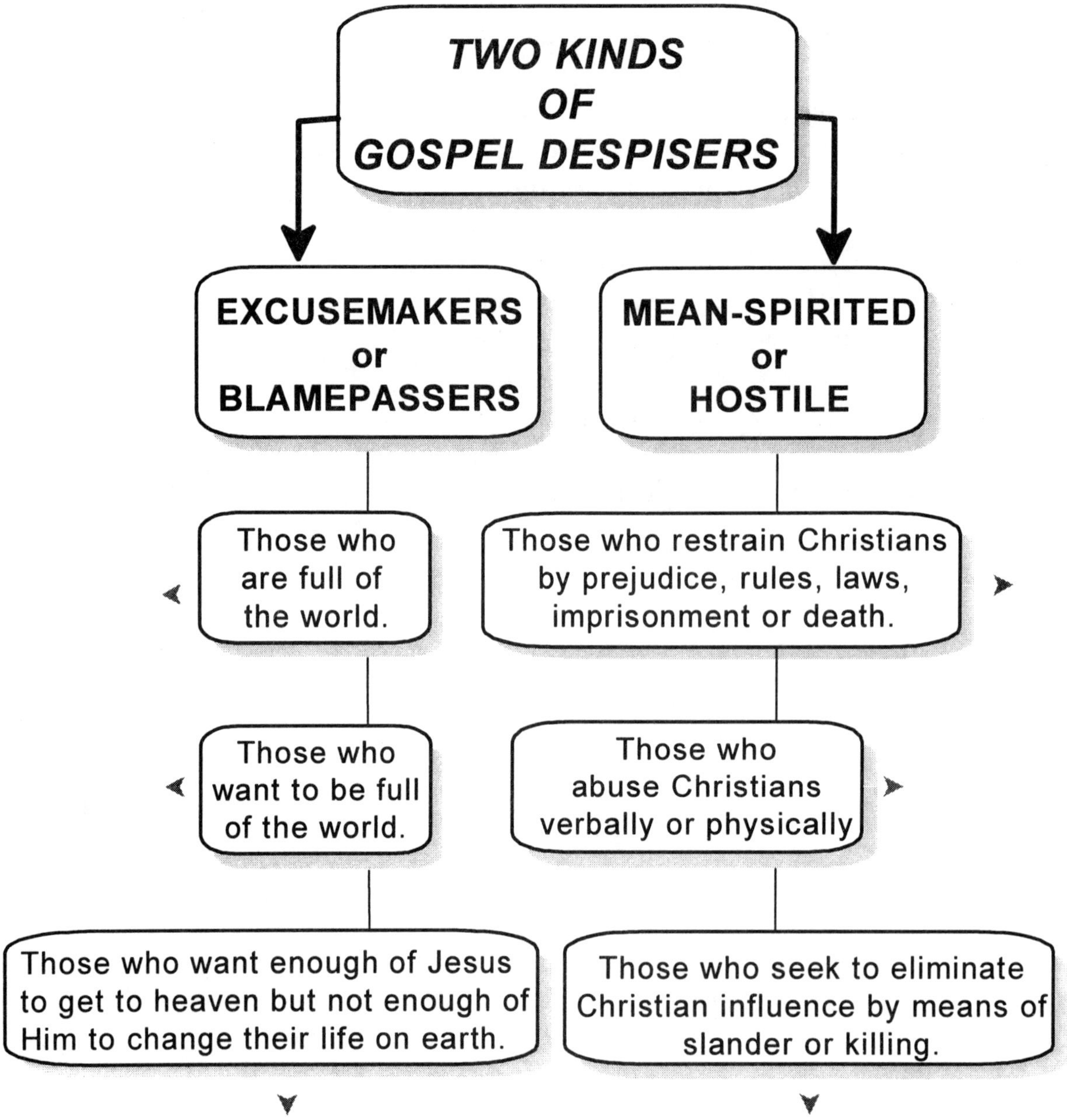
TWO KINDS OF GOSPEL DESPISERS
EXCUSEMAKERS or BLAMEPASSERS
MEAN-SPIRITED or HOSTILE
Those who are full of the world.
Those who want to be full of the world.
Those who want enough of Jesus to get to heaven but not enough of Him to change their life on earth.
Those who restrain Christians by prejudice, rules, laws, imprisonment or death.
Those who abuse Christians verbally or physically
Those who seek to eliminate Christian influence by means of slander or killing.

38. Arrows pointing outward extend from each of the classifications in the previous chart. Following is a list of parable subjects that correspond to the various classifications. Match the subjects by placing them in the margins adjacent to the arrows of the classifications to which they correspond.

rocky ground
thorny ground
hard path
weeds
foolish virgins
bad fish
lamp under a bushel
lamp under a bed
lamps low in oil
pearls before swine
person(s) without wedding garments

39. The Acts of the Apostles and later Scriptures bear abundant evidence of the three forms of outrage listed under the category *Mean-Spirited and Hostile.* In *The Parable of the King's Son's Wedding* we read that they did three things:

1.) they *took his servants,*
2.) they *treated them spitefully,*
3.) they *slew them.*

On the illustration match these three types of treatment to the corresponding classification.

40. Look up the following scriptures and match them in the margin adjacent to the corresponding category.

Acts 4:3 Acts 5:18
Acts 5:40 Acts 7:57-60
Acts 8:3 Acts 12:3
Acts 14:5,19 Acts 17:5
Acts 21:30 Acts 23:2 and Matt. 23:34

This parable concludes with the summary, *Many are called but few are chosen.* The 'called and not chosen' surely included many others that did not wholeheartedly embrace the invitation. The sifting and separating of the "chosen" from all "who are called" had been taking place long before in the Kingdom of God. It was fulfilled in the history of that entire generation which went out of Egypt -- they were all *called*, yet were not in the end *chosen to* enter the Promised Land.

41. Look up I Corinthians.10:1-10 and Heb.3:7-19. Why were so many who were called not chosen?

42. Of the twelve who were sent to see the promised land, how many were chosen? Who were they? Why were they chosen?

43. Read Judges chapter 7. How many of Gideon's army were called? How many were chosen? Why?

No doubt, this principle truth, *many are called but few are chosen*, will continue in its sifting and separating of the sincere from the insincere.

4

Meanwhile, Back on the Farm

Returning to the analogy of the farm as found not only in the key parable, *The Parable of the Sower*, but repeatedly throughout Scripture, let's look at a few choice words from John the Baptist found in Matthew Chapter 3 verses 7-12.

1. Read Matthew 3:7-12. What does John say and to whom in verses 8, 9?

2. Whom do you think John the Baptist might say this to today?

3. In verses 11, 12 we know John was referring to the initial coming of Jesus. What did John say He would do upon arrival? What would He carry?

The winnowing fork, or fan, is similar in design to a long-pronged rake or pitchfork. It was used to toss harvested grain into the wind whereupon the residue blew away while the grain, being heavier, would drop back to the ground. The grain was sometimes sifted after the winnowing (Luke. 22:31). This was the primary method of separating the tares and chaff from the grain. The chaff then was burned but the grain was stored.

John refers to the winnowing fork as being carried by Jesus upon His first coming. This declaration carries interesting implications.

4. What does John declare Jesus will do with the winnowing fork?

5. Compare John the Baptist's words in Matthew 3:11, 12 to Jesus' description of the reaping at harvest time in

   ... *The Parable of the Sower*
   Matthew 13:27-30

   ... *The Parable of the Tares*
   Matthew 13:41-43

   ... *The Parable of the Net*
   Matthew 13:48-50.

   ...Other Biblical pictures concerning *winnowing and judgment.*
   Job 21:18
   Psalm 1:3,4
   Isaiah 29:5
   Isaiah 41:16
   Daniel 2:35

6. What does John warn his audience of in Matthew 3:10?

☞ The fact that the ax is openly laid at the root of the tree, in plain view for all to see, is indicative of two important characteristics of God:

1.) Extreme lovingkindness, longsuffering and patience (not wanting any to perish but all to come to repentance).
2.) Justice (or fairness) which requires a solemn impending judgment and its consequences for all who refuse or neglect to accept His invitation and order their lives accordingly.

God *yearns patiently* for all men to be saved and bring forth fruit unto repentance and he is granting "whosoever will" an extended period of mercy and grace that they might turn from lives of selfish preoccupation to new life in Him.

The ax, openly lying unwielded but ready for use, is also evidence that there will be no justifiable excuse or reason for surprise when the time arrives for "cutting down non-bearing fruit trees." Why? Because all have been invited, all have been warned, and all have been given ample time and an ample way of escape through exercise of faith in Christ.

As we bring our study in unlocking Christ's parables to a close we must not neglect to examine ourselves, lest we should be left crying "Lord, Lord," after the time allotted for His longsuffering, patience closes and the door to Heaven is shut.

When the final call was heard, *all arose, and trimmed their lamps* in an attempt at preparation. Everyone eventually intends to seriously search his life concerning whether he will receive praise from God. Many like to gamble, putting off this examination to the last possible moment, but beyond the day of judgment it cannot be delayed. "When the day of Christ comes, a flood of light shall pour into the darkest corners of all hearts, so that self-deception will be no longer possible."[1]

Analyzation of our inner hearts is a delicate, critical process. The extent of our heart's condition and whether the ax will one day be wielded upon us can be found "in the branches of the tree."

Is there fruit? If no, why not, and if yes, is it quality fruit or wild?

Before proceeding, pause and analyze your own heart once again.

All Christ's parables have a certain unity and natural order. In the *Sower* we saw the resistance and neglect which the Gospel meets in the world, but that planting and reproducing the gospel in others is a non-optional condition and true evidence of being a *real* Christian.

In the *Tares*, other obstacles to the *internal* development of Christ's kingdom are traced to the Satanic Planter, and a clear warning against premature separation made by us prior to the harvest.

The next parables outline every individual's relation to the kingdom. Specific focus is on those who have discovered the worth of the kingdom. These parables show that such people will gladly renounce all things for the sake of the kingdom and press forward in this present time of grace to be found among those who shall be the Lord's.

All the parables we covered were in ways prophetic, for they foretold things that will come to pass.

Whenever we ponder Christ's parables, we must always be careful to remember that though they overflow with wisdom concerning life and death, heaven and hell, the Second Coming, salvation, guidelines for living, and more, it was not the Lord's main purpose in His parables to acquaint us with the future destinies of his church or hidden mysteries in His word, but rather to give practical rules and warnings for conduct and purpose in life.

7. Considering the final statement in the last paragraph above along with all you have learned concerning Christ's parables, what are the predominant essential truths you have gained from completing this workbook on Christ's parables? How will this effect your life from here on?

Appendix
Points on the Parables of Jesus

1.) A parable is a short story that is practical to everyday life, but intended to convey spiritual truths. It can have a thousand applications but only one true meaning and focus. In other words, a parable compares spiritual truths with common experiences in life.

A recognized authority on the Lord's parables, R.C. Trench, explains them as follows: The parable differs from the fable by moving in a spiritual world, and never transgressing the actual order of things natural. It differs from the proverb in being a narrative, from the fable in being true to nature, from the myth in being undeceptive, from the allegory in that it veils the spiritual truth.[1]

2.) Christ's parables are a standard for rightly dividing Truth. Though threaded with the social and cultural practices of their time, the parables are vital today. They serve as finely woven screens (paradigms) through which we can sift our spiritual beliefs to detect error or accuracy. Jesus' parables were never intended for developing doctrine. They are simply to be used as a standard for reliably testing our doctrine.

3.) Each parable carries only one essential meaning. Though a parable may have thousands of applications, each one has a singular focus with all of its detail pointing to that meaning. The number of sermons born from "The Parable of the Sower" demonstrates the capacity for multiple applications but it is important that we align those applications with the intended single focus in order to achieve an accurate interpretation.

4.) The true interpretation of Christ's parables is not always easily discovered, but upon discovery, it is always easy! One has usually found the right interpretation of a parable if it leaves none of the main circumstances unexplained. How much information is significant in each parable?-- all of it!

5.) Two purposes of parables: Revelation and concealment. The meaning of each of the Lord's parables is intentionally concealed; like a butterfly in a cocoon it is wrapped in the story-line, unapparent to the casual onlooker. Yet the meaning is clearly revealed to the sincere of heart. This is an amazing accomplishment of two diametrically opposed goals within the same parable unit: a feat which leads us to praise the excellence of Divine Wisdom at work.

---

1. R.C. Trench, *Notes on the Parables of Our Lord*, (Grand Rapids, Michigan: Baker Book House, 1980), p. 5.

6.) "Popularity"[1] disqualifies an interpretation from being wholly accurate. "Popularity" of an interpretation is sound evidence that something somewhere has been misconstrued. This warning is commonly ignored.

One of the greatest Bible expositors of the 20th century, Dr. G. Campbell Morgan, said, "We must be set free from *the bondage of popular and traditional views in interpretation.*" Echoing his concern, Dr. R. A. Torrey has said that if some Bible Teachers were practicing law and interpreting it as they interpret the Bible, they would be laughed out of court.

So why are so many of us still trudging about in the mud of popular interpretations instead of a more Biblically clear view? Largely, two reasons:

a) An ongoing temptation to excuse or overlook the sinful inadequacies in ourselves and others.

b) When teaching there lurks a grave temptation toward *excessive fondness for injecting personal experience and ingenuity.* Inserting personal wit and experience often clouds the truth rather than enhancing it.

Though all of us must guard against this temptation, it must be fought more severely by Bible teachers, students, and clergy, because their roles make them especially prone to this temptation.

We must remember our goal is not to glorify ourselves through clever stories and insight, nor to make our hearers feel comfortable by giving them excuses for their sin. The goal is the sanctification of the heart through truth--whether the truth proves to be pleasant or painful depends mainly on the hearer's response.

1. *Popular* in this context does not mean the commonalty of an interpretation but rather the appeal of an interpretation. If the interpretation is appealing to nearly everyone then there is something inherently wrong with that interpretation.